JN090710

IBC対訳ライブラリー

英語で読む
オー・ヘンリー傑作短篇集

The Best Short Stories of O. Henry

著=**オー・ヘンリー**
英語解説=**田畑則重**

イラスト ＝ Tomoko Taguchi
日本語訳 ＝ 森安真知子

本書の英語テキストは、弊社から刊行されたラダーシリーズレベル2
『*O. Henry's American Scenes* オー・ヘンリー傑作短編集』から転載しています。

目　次

Biography of O. Henry

In 1910 a man named William Sidney Porter died in New York of cirrhosis of the liver. He was a heavy drinker. Years earlier he had spent time in prison for embezzlement after attempting to evade arrest by fleeing to Honduras. His death would not have attracted much attention if his pen name had not been O. Henry, the greatest short story writer of his day.

Porter was born in North Carolina in 1862, his father a physician. His mother died of tuberculosis when he was three. Porter attended an elementary school run by his aunt, who would continue to tutor him until he was fifteen, and he also went to high school. He was a voracious reader, going through whatever he could get his hands on. In 1879 he was working in his uncle's drugstore and in 1881, at the age of 19, became a licensed pharmacist.

In 1882 he traveled to Texas with an acquaintance, thinking the drier air would cure a persistent cough. He lived on a sheep ranch and worked as a babysitter, ranch hand, shepherd, and cook. In 1884 he made a trip to the state capital, Austin, which he liked so much he decided to stay. While there, he worked at a number of jobs, including pharmacist, bank teller, and draftsman. On the side, he began writing stories.

While in Austin he joined several musical groups——he could sing and play the guitar and mandolin. In the course

オー・ヘンリーの生涯

　1910年ニューヨークで、ウィリアム・シドニー・ポーターという男が肝硬変のため亡くなった。彼は大酒飲みだった。数年前まで彼は横領罪で刑務所に入っていた。それもホンジュラスへの逃亡を試みた末のことだ。もし彼のペンネームが当時もっとも偉大な短編作家、オー・ヘンリーでなければ、その死が世間に注目されることはなかったであろう。

　ポーターは1862年にノースカロライナ州で医師の息子として生まれた。母親は彼が3歳のときに結核で亡くなった。叔母が運営する小学校へ入学し、15歳までその叔母に教育をうけ、さらに高校へも進学した。非常に熱心な読書家で、どんな本であれ手に入ったものを読みあさった。1879年から彼は叔父の薬屋で働き、1881年に19歳で薬剤師となった。

　1882年にポーターは知人とテキサス州を旅した。乾燥した空気が長引く咳を癒してくれるのではと考えたのだ。彼は羊牧場で生活し、子守、牧場作業員、羊番、料理人として働いた。1884年にテキサスの州都オースティンまで出かけると、そこを非常に気に入り、留まることを決めた。そこでは、薬剤師、銀行出納係、製図技師など、数々の職に携わることになるが、そのかたわらで、執筆を始めた。

　オースティンにいる間、いくつかの音楽グループに参加した。歌がうまく、ギターやマンドリンの演奏もできたのだ。やがて彼

of time, he met the 17-year-old Athol Estes and immediately fell in love. Her family objected, saying she had tuberculosis, but in 1887 the two eloped and were married. In 1889 they were blessed with a daughter after a first child, a son, had died shortly after birth.

In 1891 Porter took up work at the First National Bank of Austin as a teller and bookkeeper. In 1894 he was accused of embezzlement and resigned. It is unclear whether he actually embezzled or it was simply a matter of sloppy bookkeeping.

He then began to devote himself to a humorous weekly magazine he had started while working at the bank. It was called The Rolling Stone, and contained a good deal of satire and Porter's own short stories and sketches. Although it attained a circulation of 1,500, that wasn't enough to support his family, and the magazine folded in 1895.

Not all was lost, however, for the magazine had caught the attention of an editor at the Houston Post. In order to be more conveniently located for his work at the Post, Porter moved his family to Houston. His starting salary was low but gradually rose as his writings became more widely followed. It was here that he developed a habit that would serve him well throughout his career: he hung out in hotel lobbies talking to people, observing them, gaining ideas for his writing.

In was at this point, in 1896, just as things seemed to be looking up, that federal auditors discovered the earlier case of alleged embezzlement and arrested him. Out on bail and on his way to the courthouse for trial, he decided on a whim to

は17歳のアトール・エストスと出会い、恋に落ちる。アトールの家族は、彼女は結核を患っているからと反対するが、1887年に2人は駆け落ちし、結婚した。長男は生後まもなく亡くなったが、1889年に娘を授かった。

　1891年にポーターはオースティンのファースト・ナショナル銀行で出納係兼、簿記係としての仕事を始めるが、1894年、横領の罪に問われ、辞職した。実際に横領をしたのか、単にずさんな簿記による問題だったのかはわかっていない。

　ポーターは銀行で働きながら創刊した、風刺週刊紙に専念しはじめた。『ローリングストーン』という雑誌で、風刺の利いた文章と、ポーター自身による短編やスケッチを掲載し、1500部を発行したが、家族を養うには十分でなく、1895年に廃刊となった。

　しかし、すべてを失ったわけではなかった。その雑誌は『ヒューストン・ポスト』の編集者の注意を引いたのだ。『ヒューストン・ポスト』での仕事の利便性のため、ポーターは家族とヒューストンへ移った。初任給は低かったが、彼の文章が広く注目されるにつれ徐々に昇給する。ここで作家としてその後も役立つ習慣を身につけた。ホテルのロビーをうろついては人々と会話し、観察し、小説のアイデアを得たのだ。

　この時点では事態は良い方へ向かうように思われたが、1896年に連邦会計監査官がかつて申し立てられた横領事件を見つけ、ポーターを逮捕した。保釈されたポーターはしかし、公判のために裁判所に向かう途中、出来心から国外逃亡を決意する。ホンジュラスで数ヵ月経った頃、再会を夢見ていた妻アトールが死の

flee the country. After spending several months in Honduras where he hoped to meet up with his wife, he learned that Athol was dying. He had no choice but to return and surrender himself to the authorities.

Athol died in 1897, and Porter was convicted of embezzlement in 1898, with a sentence of five-years imprisonment. As a licensed pharmacist, he was lucky enough to work in the prison hospital. He even had a room to himself, not a prison cell. Here he continued to write, producing 14 stories, which were published under various pseudonyms, one of which was O. Henry. In 1901, after three years of incarceration, Porter was released early for good behavior.

In 1902 Porter moved to New York City, which marked the beginning of his most prolific period as a writer. New York saw him write 381 short stories, many of them for the New York World Sunday Magazine. His fans were many, his critics few. He remarried in 1907, but found himself alone again in 1909. He died in 1910 and was buried in Riverside Cemetery, Ashville, North Carolina.

床についていることを知る。帰国せざるを得なくなったポーター
は、司法にその身を委ねることになる。

　1897年にアトールが亡くなると、ポーターは1898年に横領で
有罪となり、禁固5年の判決を受けた。幸い薬剤師の資格があっ
たので、刑務所内の病院で働いた。独房ではなく、個室を持つ
こともできた。そこで執筆を続け、14編の作品を書き上げた。そ
れらは様々な筆名で出版されたが、その中のひとつがオー・ヘン
リーだった。3年間拘留された後、1901年、品行方正により早期
釈放となった。

　1902年、ポーターはニューヨーク市へ移り、作家として最も多
くの作品を生み出し始める。ニューヨークでは381編の短編を書き、
その多くは『ニューヨーク・
ワールド・サンデー・マガ
ジン』に掲載された。多く
のファンに支持され、批判
する人はほとんどいなかっ
た。1907年に再婚するが、
1909年に離婚。1910年、そ
の生涯を閉じ、ノースカロ
ライナ州アッシュビルのリ
バーサイド墓地に埋葬され
る。

本書の構成

本書は、

□ 英日対訳による本文　　　□ 欄外の語注
□ ストーリーごとのフレーズ解説　　□ MP3形式の英文音声

で構成されています。本書は、やさしい英語で書かれたオー・ヘンリーの短篇とその日本語訳を読み進めることで、ストーリーを楽しみながら、同時に役に立つ英語フレーズも習得できるようになっています。

英文ページのQRコードをスマートフォンなどで読み取ると、そこからの英文テキストの音声を聞くことができます。また、PCなどに一括でダウンロードすることもできますので、発音を確認しながら読むことができます。

＊本書は左ページに英語、右ページに日本語を配し、対照して読み進めていただけるようつくられています。必ずしも同じ位置から始めることは難しいのですが、なるべく該当の日本語が見つけられやすいように、ところどころ行をあけるなどして調整してあります。

●音声一括ダウンロード●

本書の朗読音声（MP3形式）を下記URLとQRコードからPCなどに一括ダウンロードすることができます。

https://ibcpub.co.jp/audio_dl/0800/

※ダウンロードしたファイルはZIP形式で圧縮されていますので、解凍ソフトが必要です。

※MP3ファイルを再生するには、iTunes（Apple Music）やWindows Media Playerなどのアプリケーションが必要です。

※PCや端末、ソフトウェアの操作・再生方法については、編集部ではお答えできません。付属のマニュアルやインターネットの検索を利用するか、開発元にお問い合わせください。

The Best
Short Stories of
O. Henry

オー・ヘンリー傑作短篇集

The Gift of the Magi

マギの贈り物

One dollar and eighty-seven cents. That was all. She had put it aside, one cent and then another and then another, in her careful buying of meat and other food. Della counted it three times. One dollar and eighty-seven cents. And the next day would be Christmas.

There was nothing to do but fall on the bed and cry. So Della did.

While the lady of the home is slowly growing quieter, we can look at the home. Furnished rooms at a cost of eight dollars a week. There is little more to say about them.

In the hall below was a letter-box too small to hold a letter. There was an electric bell, but it could not make a sound. Also there was a name beside the door: "Mr. James Dillingham Young."

■put ～ aside ～を取っておく　■and then another さらにもう1つ　■There was nothing to do but ～．～以外することがなかった　■grow quiet 落ち着く ■furnished 形 家具つきの　■little more ほとんどもうない

1ドルと87セント。これですべて。デラは、肉などの食料品を買うときも余分な出費をしないようにして注意して、1セント、1セントと貯めてきたのだった。3回数えた。1ドルと87セント。明日はクリスマスというのに。

　デラはベッドに倒れこんでただ泣くしかない。そして、そうしたのだ。

　この家の女主人が落ち着くまでに、家を見ることにしよう。家具付きで、1週間につき8ドルの家賃。部屋についてはこれ以上言うことはない。

　階下の入り口には、郵便受けがあるが、小さすぎて手紙が入らない。呼び鈴はあっても、音が鳴らない。さらに、ドアの脇にはMr. James Dillingham Youngと名前が記されている。

When the name was placed there, Mr. James Dillingham Young was being paid thirty dollars a week. Now, when he was being paid only twenty dollars a week, the name seemed too long and important. It should perhaps have been "Mr. James D. Young." But when Mr. James Dillingham Young entered the furnished rooms, his name became very short indeed. Mrs. James Dillingham Young put her arms warmly about him and called him "Jim." You have already met her. She is Della.

Della finished her crying and cleaned the marks of it from her face. She stood by the window and looked out with no interest. Tomorrow would be Christmas Day, and she had only one dollar and eighty-seven cents with which to buy Jim a gift. She had put aside as much as she could for months, with this result. Twenty dollars a week is not much. Everything had cost more than she had expected. It always happened like that.

Only one dollar and eighty-seven cents to buy a gift for Jim. Her Jim. She had had many happy hours planning something nice for him. Something nearly good enough. Something almost worth the honor of belonging to Jim.

■put one's arms about ～に腕をまわす ■with no interest 無関心に ■put aside ～を取っておく ■as much as one can できる限り ■worth 動 ～の価値がある

その場所に名前が置かれたとき、ジェームズ・ディリンガム・ヤング氏は1週間あたり30ドルの給料をとっていた。1週間あたり20ドルしかもらっていない今となると、ドアの脇の名前は、いたずらに長ったらしく、仰々しく思えてくる。おそらく、Mr. James D. Youngとすればよかったのだ。だが、ジェームズ・ディリンガム・ヤング氏がこの家具付きの部屋に入ったときには、彼の名前はひどく短くなった。ジェームズ・ディリンガム・ヤング夫人がやさしく彼の背に腕をまわし、ジムと呼んだのだ。読者は、夫人にすでに会っている。つまり、デラがヤング夫人なのだ。

デラは泣きやみ、顔から涙のあとを拭き取った。窓の脇に立ち、ぼんやりと外を眺めた。明日はクリスマス。それなのにデラには1ドルと87セントしかない。それでジムへのプレゼントを買わなければならないのだ。デラは数ヵ月のあいだ、できるだけ節約をして金をためてきた。その結果がこれだ。1週間あたり20ドルはたいした金額ではない。そのうえ、すべてのものが予想外に高かった。こういうことはよく起ることである。

ジムのプレゼントを買うのにたった1ドルと87セントしかない。「わたしのジム」。デラは、ジムになにか素敵なものを買おうと計画し、何時間も何時間も幸せな時間を過ごしてきた。なにかとても素敵なもの、ジムが持つことで名誉になるものをだ。

There was a looking-glass between the windows of the room. Perhaps you have seen the kind of looking-glass that is placed in eight-dollar, furnished rooms. It was very narrow. A person could see only a little of himself at a time. However, if he was very thin and moved very quickly, he might be able to get a good view of himself. Della, being quite thin, had mastered this art.

Suddenly she turned from the window and stood before the glass. Her eyes were shining brightly, but her face had lost its color. Quickly she pulled down her hair and let it fall to its complete length.

The James Dillingham Youngs were very proud of two things which they owned. One thing was Jim's gold watch. It had once belonged to his father. And, long ago, it had belonged to his father's father. The other thing was Della's hair.

If a queen had lived in the rooms near theirs, Della would have washed and dried her hair where the queen could see it. Della knew her hair was more beautiful than any queen's jewels and gifts.

■looking-glass 图 鏡　■at a time 一度に　■get a good view of ～がよく見える
■art 图 技術　■be proud of ～を自慢に思う　■If A had ～ ed, B would have …ed.
もしAが～していたら、Bは…しただろう

部屋の窓と窓とのあいだには鏡があった。家具付きで8ドルの部屋に備えつけられる類の鏡といえば、どんなものかはおおよそ想像がつくだろう。ひどく幅の狭い鏡である。姿を映そうとしても、その鏡には身体のほんの一部しか映らない。しかし、その人がとても細くて、サッと動いたら、どうにか全身を見ることができるようなしろものである。デラは、とてもほっそりしており、そのうえ鏡に姿を映すコツを習得していた。

　突然デラは窓から離れ、鏡の前に立った。目はきらきらと輝いていたが、顔に血の気はなかった。素早く髪を下ろし、髪が完全にその長さになるにまかせた。

　ジェームズ・ディリンガム・ヤング夫妻には、誇れるものが二つあった。一つは、ジムの金時計である。それは、以前は父親のものであった。その昔には、父親の父親が所有していた。もう一つは、デラの髪であった。

　女王という身分の人が近くの部屋に住んでいるようなことがあれば、デラは洗った髪を、わざと女王が見えるような場所で乾かしたであろう。デラは自分の髪が、女王のどの宝石や贈り物より美しいと知っていた。

If a king had lived in the same house, with all his riches, Jim would have looked at his watch every time they met. Jim knew that no king had anything so valuable.

So now Della's beautiful hair fell about her, shining like a falling stream of brown water. It reached below her knee. It almost made itself into a dress for her.

And then she put it up on her head again, nervously and quickly. Once she stopped for a moment and stood still while a tear or two ran down her face.

She put on her old brown coat. She put on her old brown hat. With the bright light still in her eyes, she moved quickly out the door and down to the street.

Where she stopped, the sign said: "Mrs. Sofronie. Hair Articles of All Kinds."

Up to the second floor Della ran, and stopped to get her breath.

Mrs. Sofronie, large, too white, cold-eyed, looked at her.

"Will you buy my hair?" asked Della.

"I buy hair," said Mrs. Sofronie. "Take your hat off and let me look at it."

Down fell the brown waterfall.

■make A into ~ Aを~に仕立て上げる　■a A or two　1つか2つのA　■put on 身につける　■of all kinds あらゆる種類の　■get one's breath 息を整える　■Down fall the brown waterfall.《副詞を強調する倒置構文》

もし王という身分の人が全財産を持って同じ建物に住んでいるとしたら、ジムは彼に会うたびに自分の時計を見つめただろう。ジムは、いかなる王であれ、自分の時計に匹敵するほど価値のあるものを持っているはずがない、と思っていた。

　このとき、デラの美しい髪はデラの身体を包み、それはまるで茶色の一筋の流れ落ちる水のように輝いていた。髪はデラの膝の下まで達し、デラのためにあつらえたドレスのようだった。

　それから、デラはあわてて手早く髪を結いあげた。それからちょっと手を休め、じっと立ったまま、一筋、二筋と涙を流した。

　デラは古びた茶色のコートを着て、やはり古びた茶色の帽子をかぶった。目にきらきらした輝きを残して、急いで外に出て、通りを歩いて行った。

　デラは、「ミセス・ソフロニーの店。頭髪用品を取りそろえています」と書かれた看板があるところで立ち止まった。

　2階に駆け上がってから、息を整えた。

　ミセス・ソフロニーは大柄な女性で、その肌の色は白すぎるほど白くて、冷たい目つきをしていた。彼女はデラを見つめた。

　「わたしの髪を買っていただけません?」デラは言った。

　「髪は買うよ。帽子をとって、髪を見せておくれな」

　茶色の滝が流れ落ちた。

"Twenty dollars," said Mrs. Sofronie, lifting the hair to feel its weight.

"Give it to me quick," said Della.

Oh, and the next two hours seemed to fly. She was going from one shop to another, to find a gift for Jim.

She found it at last. It surely had been made for Jim and no one else. There was no other like it in any of the shops, and she had looked in every shop in the city.

It was a gold watch chain, very simply made. Its value was in its rich and pure material. Because it was so plain and simple, you knew that it was very valuable. All good things are like this.

It was good enough for The Watch.

As soon as she saw it, she knew that Jim must have it. It was like him. Quietness and value——Jim and the chain both had quietness and value. She paid twenty-one dollars for it. And she hurried home with the chain and eighty-seven cents.

With that chain on his watch, Jim could look at his watch and learn the time anywhere he might be. Though the watch was so fine, it had never had a fine chain. He sometimes took it out and looked at it only when no one could see him do it.

■seem to ～のように思われる　■from one ～ to another ～から～に次々と　■no one else 他の誰として～ない　■learn the time 時間を知る　■though 腰 ～にも関わらず　■take out 取り出す

「20ドルだね」重さを計るように髪を持ち上げながら、ミセス・ソフロニーは言った。

「すぐ、そのお金を下さいな」デラは叫んだ。

ああ、それからの2時間は飛ぶように過ぎていった。デラは、ジムへのプレゼントを探すために、店から店へと歩き回った。

やっとそのものを見つけたのだ。そのものは、ほかの誰のためでもない、まさにジムのために作られているようだった。どこの店にもそういったものが見当たらず、デラは街中の店を探しまわったのだ。

それは、時計の、きわめて単純なつくりの金の鎖であった。その値打ちは、混じりけのない材料がたっぷりと使われているところにあった。その金の鎖はとてもシンプルなので、それだけで値打ちがあることがわかった。価値あるものは、すべてこのようなものなのだ。

その金の鎖は、ジムの時計によく合いそうだった。

デラはその金の鎖を目にするなり、これはジムが持つべきものであると直感した。金の鎖はジムのようだった。目立たず価値があること——ジムも鎖もまさにこのようだった。デラは鎖に21ドル支払い、鎖と87セントを手にして大急ぎで家に戻った。

時計にこの鎖をつけたら、ジムはどこにいても、時計を見て時間を知ることができるだろう。時計は、それは素晴らしいものだが、一度たりともそれにふさわしい鎖をつけたことがなかった。ジムは、周りに人の目がないときだけ、ときどき時計をとりだして眺めるのだった。

02

When Della arrived home, her mind quieted a little. She began to think more reasonably. She started to try to cover the sad marks of what she had done. Love and large-hearted giving, when added together, can leave deep marks. It is never easy to cover these marks, dear friends——never easy.

Within forty minutes her head looked a little better. With her short hair, she looked wonderfully like a schoolboy. She stood at the looking-glass for a long time.

"If Jim doesn't kill me," she said to herself, "before he looks at me a second time, he'll say I look like a girl who sings and dances for money. But what could I do——oh! what could I do with a dollar and eighty-seven cents?"

At seven, Jim's dinner was ready for him.

Jim was never late. Della held the watch chain in her hand and sat near the door where he always entered. Then she heard his step in the hall and her face lost color for a moment. She often said little prayers quietly, about simple everyday things. And now she said: "Please God, make him think I'm still pretty."

■mark 傷跡　■dear friends 親愛なる友よ《親しみを込めた呼びかけ》　■wonderfully 副 見事なまでに　■lose color 青ざめる　■make A think Aに〜だと思わせる

デラは家に着くと少し落ち着きを取り戻し、冷静に物事を考え始めた。自分の行為によるみじめな痕跡を隠す算段を始めた。愛と気前のいい贈り物、この二つが一緒になると簡単には消せない深い傷跡を残すものなのだ。こういった傷跡は、決して容易に隠し通せるものではない。読者諸君、決して簡単には隠せないのだ。

　40分もしないうちに、頭はいくらかましに見えるようになった。ショートヘアにすると、デラは見事に少年っぽく見えた。彼女は長い時間鏡の前に立っていた。

　「ジムがわたしを一目見ただけで殺さなければ、もう一度見る前に彼はわたしのことをお金のために歌ったり踊ったりする女の子みたいだ、って言うでしょうね。だけど、わたしに何ができたというの。1ドルと87セントで何ができたというの?」デラはひとりごちた。

　7時、ジムの夕食の用意ができた。

　ジムは決して遅れることがなかった。デラは鎖を手にして、彼がいつも入って来るドアの近くに腰を下ろした。そのとき廊下でジムの足音がした。一瞬、デラは蒼白になった。彼女はよく、ささいな日常の物事に対して短い祈りの言葉をそっと口にしていた。そして今、デラはこう祈ったのだ。「神様、どうかジムに、今でもわたしが美しいと思わせてください」

The door opened and Jim stepped in. He looked very thin and he was not smiling. Poor fellow, he was only twenty-two——and with a family to take care of! He needed a new coat and he had nothing to cover his cold hands.

Jim stopped inside the door. He was as quiet as a hunting dog when it is near a bird. His eyes looked strangely at Della, and there was an expression in them that she could not understand. It filled her with fear. It was not anger, nor surprise, nor anything she had been ready for. He simply looked at her with that strange expression on his face.

Della went to him.

"Jim, dear," she cried, "don't look at me like that. I had my hair cut off and sold it. I couldn't live through Christmas without giving you a gift. My hair will grow again. You won't care, will you? My hair grows very fast. It's Christmas, Jim. Let's be happy. You don't know what a nice——what a beautiful nice gift I got for you."

"You've cut off your hair?" asked Jim slowly. He seemed to labor to understand what had happened. He seemed not to feel sure he knew.

■poor fellow　かわいそうに《同情のつぶやき》　■take care of　～の面倒を見る　■fill A with ～　Aを～でいっぱいにする　■live through　やり過ごす　■labor to do　～しようと苦心する　■feel sure　確信する

ドアが開いてジムが入ってきた。ジムはひどくやせて見え、微笑んではいなかった。可哀そうに、弱冠22歳なのに養わなければならない家族がいる。新しいコートは必要だし、冷たい手を覆うものも持っていないのだ。

　ジムはドアの内側で立ち止まった。鳥に近づいた猟犬のように物音をたてなかった。奇妙な目つきでデラを見つめた。ジムの目に浮かんだ表情はデラには理解しがたかった。それはデラを恐怖に陥れた。怒りでも、驚きでもない。彼女があらかじめ考えていたどれにもあたらなかった。ジムはただ奇妙な表情を浮かべてデラを見つめていた。

　デラはジムの方へ歩み寄った。
　「ジム」デラは叫んだ。「そんな風にわたしを見ないで。髪を切ってもらって、売ったの。あなたにプレゼントをしないでクリスマスを過ごすなんてこと、とてもできなかったの。髪はまた伸びてくるわ。あなたは気にしないでしょう？　私の髪の毛は伸びるのが早いのよ。クリスマスよ、ジム。楽しみましょう。あなたのために、どんなに素敵な——素晴らしくきれいなプレゼントを買ったのかわかる？」
　「きみは髪を切ったんだね」ジムはゆっくりと言った。起きたことを理解しようと努めている様子であった。しかと理解しているようではなかった。

"Cut it off and sold it," said Della. "Don't you like me now? I'm me, Jim. I'm the same without my hair."

Jim looked around the room.

"You say your hair is gone?" he said.

"You don't have to look for it," said Della. "It's sold, I tell you—sold and gone, too. It's the night before Christmas, boy. Be good to me, because I sold it for you. Maybe the hairs of my head could be counted," she said, "but no one could ever count my love for you. Shall we eat dinner, Jim?"

Jim put his arms around his Della. For ten seconds let us look in another direction. Eight dollars a week or a million dollars a year—how different are they? Someone may give you an answer, but it will be wrong. The magi brought valuable gifts, but that was not among them. My meaning will be explained soon.

From inside his coat, Jim took something tied in paper. He threw it upon the table.

"I want you to understand me, Dell," he said. "Nothing like a haircut could make me love you any less. But if you'll open that, you may know what I felt when I came in."

■gone 彫 消失した ■look for ～を探す ■boy 圃 ねえ ■Be good to me. やさしくしてください ■Shall we ～？ ～しましょうよ ■Nothing makes ～ any less. ～が弱まることはない

「切って、売ったの」デラが言った。「いまのわたしが好きではないの?わたしはわたしなの、ジム。髪がなくても同じわたしなの」

ジムは部屋を見回した。

「髪の毛がなくなったというのか?」

「髪を探すなんてことはしないで。売ったと言ったでしょう。売ってなくなってしまったの。クリスマスイブなのよ。あなたのために髪を売ったの。だから、とやかく言わないでね。髪は数えることができるかもしれないけど、あなたへのわたしの愛は、絶対に誰にも数えることができないわ。夕食にしましょうよ、ジム」

ジムはデラを抱きしめた。10秒ほどほかのところに目を移してみよう。1週間に8ドルと1年間に100万ドル、これらのあいだにはどんな違いがあるのだろうか?　答える人がいるかもしれない。だが、その答えは正しくないだろう。マギは貴重な贈り物を持ってきたが、答えはその贈り物の中にはなかった。ここで言いたいことは、後ほどわかるだろう。

ジムはコートの内側から紙にくるんだものを取り出し、テーブルの上に投げ置いた。

「きみにはわかってほしいんだデル。髪を切ったからといって、ぼくの君への愛はいささかも傷つくことはないとね。だけど、その包みを開けると、ぼくが部屋に入って来たときどう思ったかがわかるよ」

White fingers pulled off the paper. And then a cry of joy; and then a change to tears.

For there lay The Combs——the combs that Della had seen in a shop window and loved for a long time. Beautiful combs, with jewels, perfect for her beautiful hair. She had known they cost too much for her to buy them. She had looked at them without the least hope of owning them. And now they were hers, but her hair was gone.

But she held them to her heart, and at last was able to look up and say: "My hair grows so fast, Jim!"

And then she jumped up and cried, "Oh, oh!"

Jim had not yet seen his beautiful gift. She held it out to him in her open hand. The gold seemed to shine softly as if with her own warm and loving spirit.

"Isn't it perfect, Jim? I hunted all over town to find it. You'll have to look at your watch a hundred times a day now. Give me your watch. I want to see how they look together."

Jim sat down and smiled.

■pull off 引っ張ってはぐ ■without least hope of ～に少しの希望もなく ■held ～ out ～を差し出す ■hunt 動 探す

白い指が包み紙をはがした。喜びの声があがり、それから涙に変わった。

　というのは、そこにはくし——デラが店のショーウィンドウで目にして、ずっと気に入っていたくしがあった。宝石がついた美しいくし、デラの美しい髪にピッタリのくし。そのくしはあまりに高価で、買えないことはわかっていた。そのくしが自分の所有物になるなど、これっぽちも考えず、ただくしを眺めていたのだった。いまや、くしはデラのものになったが、髪の毛がなくなってしまった。

　しかしながら、デラはくしを抱きしめて、やっとの思いでジムを見上げて「わたしの髪は早く伸びるのよ、ジム」と言うことができた。

　それから急に立ち上がり、「あっ」と叫んだ。

　ジムは、彼への素晴らしいプレゼントをまだ見ていなかったのだ。デラは、プレゼントを持った手を広げて彼の方へ差し出した。金は、デラの温かく、愛らしい心根を備えているかのように、柔らかな光を放っていた。

　「ピッタリじゃない、ジム？　街中探し回って見つけたの。1日に100回も時計を見なければならないわね。時計をかして。鎖と合わせるとどんな風になるのか見たいの」

　ジムは腰を下ろして微笑んだ。

"Della," said he, "let's put our Christmas gifts away and keep them a while. They're too nice to use now. I sold the watch to get the money to buy the combs. And now I think we should have our dinner."

The magi, as you know, were wise men——wonderfully wise men——who brought gifts to the newborn Christ child. They were the first to give Christmas gifts. Being wise, their gifts were doubtless wise ones. And here I have told you the story of two foolish children. Each sold the most valuable thing he owned in order to buy a gift for the other. But let me speak a last word to the wise of these days: Of all who give gifts, these two were the most wise. Of all who give and receive gifts, such as they are the most wise. Everywhere, they are the wisest. They are the magi.

■put ~ away ～をしまう　■too ~ to … ～すぎて…できない　■newborn 形 生まれたばかりの　■in order to ～するために　■these days 近頃、今時　■of all who ～するすべての人の中で

「デラ、クリスマスプレゼントは、しばらくそのままとっておこうよ。素晴らしすぎて、いまはとても使えないよ。ぼくは、くしを買うために時計を売ったんだ。さあ、夕食にしようよ」

　ご存知のように、マギは賢者たち、それも並外れて賢い男たちで、生まれたばかりのキリストに贈り物を携えてやって来た。彼らは、クリスマスの贈り物をした最初の人間である。マギたちは賢かった。だから彼らの贈り物が、それにふさわしいものだったことに疑いの余地はない。ここでわたしは、「愚かな若い二人」の物語を語った。それぞれが、自分が所有しているなかで一番高価なものを売って、相手へのプレゼントを買ったのだ。だが、最後に今どきの賢い者たちに一言言わせてもらうならば、プレゼントをする者たちのなかで、物語の二人のような者たちが一番の賢者である。プレゼントを交換する者たちのなかでも、このような者たちはとりわけ賢い。どこにいようと、二人のような人間は最高の賢者である。彼らがマギなのである。

覚えておきたい英語表現

　Magi（マギ）とは、本文中にも簡単な説明が出てきますが、聖書に見える Wise Men of the East（東方の三博士）のことです。キリストが生まれた時に東方から礼拝に来て、貴重な frankincense（乳香）、myrrh（没薬＝香料、薬）、gold（黄金）を贈り物としてささげたとされます。この題には、一見おろかな事をした主人公たちこそが聖なる心で尊い品を贈ろうとした真の賢者という著者の考えがこめられています。

> She had put it aside, one cent and then another and then another, in her careful buying of meat and other food. (p.14, 1-3行目)
> 彼女は、肉などの食料品を買うときも余分な出費をしないように注意して、1セント、1セントと貯めてきたのだった。

【解説】put aside には、例文のように「貯める」という意味のほかに、「片づける」とか「取り置く」という意味もあります。He put aside the book.（彼は本を脇に片づけた）

> I had my hair cut off and sold it. (p.26, 下から9-8行目)
> 私の髪を切ってもらって、売ったの。

【解説】「have＋目的語＋過去分詞」は日本人が苦手な構文の一つです。目的語が「～される」つまり主語が目的語を「～してもらった」という意味になりますね。He had his PC repaired.（彼はパソコンを修理してもらった）

I couldn't live through Christmas without giving you a gift.
（p.26, 下から8-7行目）

あなたにプレゼントをしないでクリスマスを過ごすなんてこと、とてもできなかったの。

【解説】live through…は、「～（ある時期、季節など）の終わりまで生き延びる」という意味ですから、直訳すると、「あなたにプレゼントもせずにクリスマスを過ごすなんて耐えられなかった」となります。

Cut it off and sold it.（p.28, 1行目）

切って、売ったの。

【解説】ここは素直に髪（it）を切ったという意味で良いのですが、Cut it out!という似た表現の方は、「お黙り！」あるいは「およしなさい！」という意味なので、取り違えないようにしましょう。

It's the night before Christmas, boy.（p.28, 6-7行目）

クリスマスイブなのよ。

【解説】boyは、ジムに対して「少年」と呼びかけたのではありません。ここでは間投詞という品詞として、「おっ」とか「あーあ」と驚きや落胆を表わしているのです。そうすることで、デラが叫びあるいは嘆き口調で「クリスマスイブなのよォッ！」と言っている心境が伝わってきます。

The Last Leaf

最後の一葉

03

In a small part of the city west of Washington Square, the streets have gone wild. They turn in different directions. They are broken into small pieces called "places." One street goes across itself one or two times. A painter once discovered something possible and valuable about this street. Suppose a painter had some painting materials for which he had not paid. Suppose he had no money. Suppose a man came to get the money. The man might walk down that street and suddenly meet himself coming back, without having received a cent!

This part of the city is called Greenwich Village. And to old Greenwich Village the painters soon came. Here they found rooms they liked, with good light, and at a low cost.

■streets go wild 道が無秩序に走る　■turn in （ある場所で）向きを変える　■break into ～に入り込む　■Suppose ～. 例えば～としよう。　■meet oneself ～ing ～している自分に直面する

ニューヨークのワシントン・スクエアの西にある小さな区域では、道は無秩序に走り、それぞれ勝手な方向に向かい、「——広場」という小さな場所に行きつくのだ。1本の通りは、1度ならずとも同じ通りを横切ることになる。かつてある画家は、この通りに可能性と価値を見出したのだ。ある画家が画材をいくらか手に入れて、その支払いが済んでいなかったとしたらどうだろう。彼が金を持っていなかったとしたらどうだろう。ある男がその代金を取り立てにやって来たとしたらどうだろう。その取り立て屋は、通りを歩き回ったあげく、突然、元の通りへ戻っていることに気がつくかもしれない。それも、1セントも受け取らずにだ。

　ニューヨークのこの区域はグリニッジ・ヴィレッジと呼ばれている。画家たちは、古いグリニッジ・ヴィレッジへ、はやばやと集まって来た。ここでは、採光が良くて家賃が安い、好みの部屋を見つけることができた。

Sue and Johnsy lived at the top of a building with three floors. One of these young women came from Maine; the other from California. They had met at a restaurant on Eighth Street. There they discovered that they liked the same kind of art, the same kind of food, and the same kind of clothes. So they decided to live and work together.

That was in the spring.

Toward winter a cold stranger entered Greenwich Village. No one could see him. He walked around touching one person here and another there with his icy fingers. He was a bad sickness. Doctors called him Pneumonia. On the east side of the city he hurried, touching many people; but in the narrow streets of Greenwich Village he did not move so quickly.

Mr. Pneumonia was not a nice old gentleman. A nice old gentleman would not hurt a weak little woman from California. But Mr. Pneumonia touched Johnsy with his cold fingers. She lay on her bed almost without moving, and she looked through the window at the wall of the house next to hers.

One morning the busy doctor spoke to Sue alone in the hall, where Johnsy could not hear.

■floor 名 階　■toward ～の少し前に　■stranger 名 よそ者　■no one 誰も（～ない）　■one here and another there ここで1人あちらで1人

スーとジョンジーは、3階建ての建物の最上階で暮らしていた。この二人の若い女性のうちの一人はメーン州の出身で、もう一人はカリフォルニアの出身であった。ふたりは八番街のレストランで知り合った。そのレストランで、美術や食べ物、そのうえ服の好みまでもが同じであることを知って、一緒に住んで仕事をすることにしたのだ。

　それは、春のことであった。
　冬に向かい、冷たいよそ者がグリニッジ・ヴィレッジに入り込んできた。誰も彼の姿を見ることはできない。彼は、氷のような冷たい指で、ここで一人あそこで一人と、人に触れながら歩き回っていた。彼は質の悪い病なのだ。医者は、彼をニューモニア（肺炎）と呼んでいる。彼は、人に触れながら、ニューヨークの東側を大急ぎで通り抜けた。だが、グリニッジ・ヴィレッジの狭い通りでは、ゆっくりとした足取りになった。
　ニューモニア氏は、親切な老紳士ではない。親切な老紳士なら、カリフォルニアから来たか弱い娘を傷つけたりするはずがない。だが、彼は、冷たい指でジョンジーに触れたのだ。ジョンジーは、ほとんど身動きもせずベッドに横たわり、窓越しに隣りの建物の壁を見つめていた。

　ある朝、多忙な医者が、ジョンジーに聞かれないように廊下でスーに話していた。

"She has a very small chance," he said. "She has a chance, if she wants to live. If people don't want to live, I can't do much for them. Your little lady has decided that she is not going to get well. Is there something that is troubling her?"

"She always wanted to go to Italy and paint a picture of the Bay of Naples," said Sue.

"Paint! Not paint. Is there anything worth being troubled about? A man?"

"A man?" said Sue. "Is a man worth——No, doctor. There is not a man."

"It is weakness," said the doctor. "I will do all I know how to do. But when a sick person begins to feel that he's going to die, half my work is useless. Talk to her about new winter clothes. If she were interested in the future, her chances would be better."

After the doctor had gone, Sue went into the workroom to cry. Then she walked into Johnsy's room. She carried some of her painting materials, and she was singing.

Johnsy lay there, very thin and very quiet. Her face was turned toward the window. Sue stopped singing, thinking that Johnsy was asleep.

■get well 治る、よくなる　■trouble about ～について心配する　■go to die 死ぬ
■If ～〈過去形〉, A would …. もし～だったらAは…だろう。

「ジョンジーには、わずかなチャンスしかない」。彼は言った。「もし彼女が生きたいと思えば、チャンスはあるがね。生きることを望まない人にたいして、できることはあまりないのだよ。君の小さな友だちは、快復しないと決めつけている。何か心を痛めるようなことがあるのかな?」

　「いつだってジョンジーは、イタリアに行って、ナポリ湾の絵を描きたがっていたわ」とスーは言った。

　「絵だって! 絵を描くことではないな。悩むのも当然、と思われるようなことはないのかね? 男とか」

　「男ですって? 男なら心配する価値があるのかしら、いいえ、先生。そういった男はいません」

　「問題は彼女の弱さだね。わたしとしては、できるかぎりの治療をするつもりだがね。だが、病人が死ぬことを考え始めると、治療の半分は無駄になってしまう。冬のニュー・ファッションのことなど、彼女に話してくれないか。もし、未来に関心を持つようだったら、生存のチャンスはずっとよくなるからね」

　医者が帰ると、スーは仕事部屋に入ってさめざめと泣いた。それから、ジョンジーの部屋へ行った。スーは、歌いながら画材をいくつか持ち込んだ。

　ジョンジーは、ベッドに横たわっていた。ひどくやせ細り、ひどく静かだった。顔は窓の方に向けられていた。スーは、ジョンジーが眠っているものと思い、歌うのをやめた。

Sue began to work. As she worked she heard a low sound, again and again. She went quickly to the bedside.

Johnsy's eyes were open wide. She was looking out the window and counting——counting back.

"Twelve," she said; and a little later, "eleven"; and then, "ten," and, "nine"; and then, "eight," and, "seven," almost together.

Sue looked out the window. What was there to count? There was only the side wall of the next house, a short distance away. The wall had no window. An old, old tree grew against the wall. The cold breath of winter had already touched it. Almost all its leaves had fallen from its dark branches.

"What is it, dear?" asked Sue.

"Six," said Johnsy, in a voice still lower. "They're falling faster now. Three days ago there were almost a hundred. It hurts my head to count them. But now it's easy. There goes another one. There are only five now."

"Five what, dear? Tell your Sue."

"Leaves. On the tree. When the last one falls, I must go, too. I've known that for three days. Didn't the doctor tell you?"

■again and again 何度も繰り返して ■count back 逆から数える ■dear 图 いとしい人、ねえ《親しみを込めた呼びかけ》 ■hurt 勔 ～を困らせる ■Tell your Sue. あなたのスー（＝私）に教えてちょうだい。

スーは絵を描き始めた。絵を描いている最中に、低い音を何度も耳にし、急いでジョンジーのベッドのそばに行った。

　ジョンジーが目を大きく見開き、窓の外を眺めて、数を逆から数えていたのだ。

　「12」ジョンジーは言った。少し遅れて「11」、それから「10」「9」、そして「8」「7」、ほぼ一緒に言った。

　スーは窓の外を眺めた。あそこに数えるようなものがあったかしら？少し離れたところに隣の建物の横壁があるだけだった。壁に窓はなかった。壁に向かって1本の老木が生えていた。冬の冷たい息吹は、すでに老木にも及び、ほとんどの葉が、黒ずんだ枝から散っていた。

　「どうしたの？」

　「6」さらに低い声でジョンジーは言った。「葉の落ち方が早くなったの。3日前には、葉は100枚ほどもあったわ。数えるのに頭痛がするくらいだった。それなのに、今は簡単に数えられる。また1枚落ちたわ。もう5枚しか残っていないのね」

　「何が5枚なの？　教えてちょうだい」

　「葉っぱなの。木の上のね。最後の葉が落ちるとき、わたしも死ぬのね。3日前からわかっていたの。お医者さまはそう言わなかった？」

"Oh, I never heard of such a thing," said Sue. "It doesn't have any sense in it. What does an old tree have to do with you? Or with your getting well? And you used to love that tree so much. Don't be a little fool. The doctor told me your chances for getting well. He told me this morning. He said you had very good chances! Try to eat a little now. And then I'll go back to work. And then I can sell my picture, and then I can buy something more for you to eat to make you strong."

"You don't have to buy anything for me," said Johnsy. She still looked out the window. "There goes another. No, I don't want anything to eat. Now there are four. I want to see the last one fall before night. Then I'll go, too."

"Johnsy, dear," said Sue, "will you promise me to close your eyes and keep them closed? Will you promise not to look out the window until I finish working? I must have this picture ready tomorrow. I need the light; I can't cover the window."

"Couldn't you work in the other room?" asked Johnsy coldly.

"I'd rather be here by you," said Sue. "And I don't want you to look at those leaves."

■have to do with ～と関係がある　■used to ～　よく～したものだ　■Don't be a fool. バカなまねはやめて。　■make ～ strong ～を強靭にする　■there goes ～がなくなる　■look out ～から外を見る　■have ～ ready ～を準備する　■would rather ～するほうがよい

46　The Last Leaf

「そんなこと聞いたこともないわ。ばかげてる。ジョンジー、あなたと老木はどういう関係があるの？　快復することと関係があるの？　あなたはあの木がとても気に入っていたわね。でも、ばかなことを言わないで。お医者様があなたの快復の見込みについて話してくれたわ。今朝話したのよ。あなたが元気になる見込みは十分あるって言っていた。さあ、もう少し食べてちょうだい。それからわたしは仕事に戻るわ。絵が売れたら、なにか力がつくような食べ物を買うことができるわ」

「わたしのためなら、何も買う必要はないわ」ジョンジーは言った。彼女は窓の外を見つめていた。「また1枚散ったわ。何も食べたくないの。葉は4枚しか残ってないのね。夜がくるまえに、最後の1枚が散るのを見たい。それから、わたしも死ぬの」

「ねえ、ジョンジー、目を閉じて、そのままにしているって約束してちょうだい。わたしが仕事を終えるまで、窓の外を見ないって約束して。この絵を明日までに仕上げなければならないの。灯りが必要なのだけど、窓の日よけを降ろせないわ」

「ほかの部屋で仕事をすることはできないの」ジョンジーは冷たく言った。

「あなたのそばにいたいの。葉っぱを見てほしくないの」

"Tell me as soon as you have finished," said Johnsy. She closed her eyes and lay white and still. "Because I want to see the last leaf fall. I have done enough waiting. I have done enough thinking. I want to go sailing down, down, like one of those leaves."

"Try to sleep," said Sue. "I must call Behrman to come up here. I want to paint a man in this picture, and I'll make him look like Behrman. I won't be gone a minute. Don't try to move till I come back."

04

Old Behrman was a painter who lived on the first floor of their house. He was past sixty. He had had no success as a painter. For forty years he had painted, without ever painting a good picture. He had always talked of painting a great picture, a masterpiece, but he had never yet started it.

He got a little money by letting others paint pictures of him. He drank too much. He still talked of his great masterpiece. And he believed that it was his special duty to do everything possible to help Sue and Johnsy.

■do enough ~ ing 十分に~する　■sail down 降りて行く　■without ever ~ ing 一度も~せずに　■let A do Aに~させる　■drank 動 drink（飲む）の過去形　■too much 過剰に

「仕事が終わったらすぐ教えてね」。ジョンジーはそういって言って目を閉じた。顔には血の気がなく、横たわったまま身じろぎもしなかった。「最後の葉が散るのを見たいの。十分に待ったわ。十分に考えたわ。あの葉のように、静かに降りて行きたいの」

　「とにかく眠りなさい。バーマンをここへ呼んでこなければならないの。この絵に男性をひとり描き込みたいの。その男性の様子をバーマンのようにしたいの。すぐに戻ってくるから。それまで、動かないでね」

　バーマン老人は同じ建物の一階に住む画家であった。年齢は60歳を越えていた。画家としての成功はなかった。40年間、絵を描き続けてきたが、素晴らしいと言える作品は何一つ描いたことがなかった。彼は、日頃、大傑作を描くのだと言っているが、いまだにそれを描き始める気配はなかった。
　彼は、他の画家のモデルになって少しばかりの金を稼ぎ、酒を浴びるほど飲んでいた。それでも、自分の傑作について語るのだった。それに、スーとジョンジーの助けとなるようなことをするのは、自分に課せられた特別の義務だと信じていた。

Sue found him in his dark room, and she knew that he had been drinking. She could smell it. She told him about Johnsy and the leaves on the tree. She said that she was afraid that Johnsy would indeed sail down, down like the leaf. Her hold on the world was growing weaker.

Old Behrman shouted his anger over such an idea.

"What!" he cried. "Are there such fools? Do people die because leaves drop off a tree? I have not heard of such a thing. No, I will not come up and sit while you make a picture of me. Why do you allow her to think such a thing? That poor little Johnsy!"

"She is very sick and weak," said Sue. "The sickness has put these strange ideas into her mind. Mr. Behrman, if you won't come, you won't. But I don't think you're very nice."

"This is like a woman!" shouted Behrman. "Who said I will not come? Go. I come with you. For half an hour I have been trying to say that I will come. God! This is not any place for someone so good as Johnsy to lie sick. Some day I shall paint my masterpiece, and we shall all go away from here. God! Yes."

■hold 图 しっかりつかむこと　■grow weak 弱る　■anger over 〜に対する怒り ■drop off 〜から落ちる　■put A into 〜 Aを〜に入れ込む　■This is like 〜. これ はまさに〜のようなものだ。　■God! なんてことだ！《苛立ちを表す間投詞》

老人は、自分の暗い部屋にいた。スーは、彼が酒を飲んでいたことに気がついていた。酒の匂いがしていた。スーは老人に、ジョンジーと木の葉のことを話した。「ジョンジーが、本当に木の葉のように下に落ちていくようで怖いの。この世への執着心がだんだん薄れていくようなの」

　バーマン老人は、これを聞いて、怒りのあまり叫んだ。

　「なんだって！ そんなバカ者がいるのか？ 木の葉が散ったからといって、人が死ぬのかね？ そんなバカな話、聞いたことがない。いやだね。わしは上の階には行かんよ。おまえさんが絵を描いている間、ずっと座っているなんて真っ平だね。何がまた、そんなばかげたことをジョンジーに考えさせたのかね。ああ可哀そうなジョンジー」

　「ジョンジーはひどい病気で、とても弱っている。病気がこんなおかしなことを考えさせているのよ。ところでバーマンさん、来たくないなら、来なくて結構です。でも、あなたがあまりいい人だとは思わないわ」

　「まさに女だな」バーマンはわめいた。「誰が行かないと言った？ いくさ。おまえさんと一緒に行くよ。30分間も、ずっと行くと言うつもりだったんだ。くそ！ ここは、ジョンジーのようないい娘が病気で寝込むようなところではないぞ。そのうちに、わしが傑作を描いて、みんなでここから出て行くんだ。くそ！ そうだな」

Johnsy was sleeping when they went up. Sue covered the window and took Behrman into the other room. There they looked out the window fearfully at the tree. Then they looked at each other for a moment without speaking. A cold rain was falling, with a little snow in it too.

Behrman sat down, and Sue began to paint.

She worked through most of the night.

In the morning, after an hour's sleep, she went to Johnsy's bedside. Johnsy with wide-open eyes was looking toward the window. "I want to see," she told Sue.

Sue took the cover from the window.

But after the beating rain and the wild wind that had not stopped through the whole night, there still was one leaf to be seen against the wall. It was the last on the tree. It was still dark green near the branch. But at the edges it was turning yellow with age. There it was hanging from a branch nearly twenty feet above the ground.

"It is the last one," said Johnsy. "I thought it would surely fall during the night. I heard the wind. It will fall today, and I shall die at the same time."

■go up 上がる ■take A into ~ Aを~に連れて行く ■look at each other 顔を見合わせる ■through the night 夜通し ■take A from B BからAを取る ■with age 年月を経て

二人が部屋に入ったとき、ジョンジーは眠っていた。スーは、窓の日よけを降ろしてバーマンを別の部屋に連れて行った。その部屋から恐る恐る窓の外の木を見た。それから、黙って一瞬、顔を見合わせた。雪まじりの冷たい雨が降っていた。

　バーマンは腰をおろし、スーは絵を描き始めた。
　スーは、ほとんど夜通し、ずっと絵を描いていた。
　朝、1時間ほど眠ってから、ジョンジーのベッドのそばに行った。ジョンジーは、目を開けて窓の方を見つめていた。「見たいの」スーに言った。
　スーは窓の日よけを上げた。
　だが、一晩中、やむことなく打ち付けるように雨が降り、激しい風が吹いていたにもかかわらず、壁には1枚の葉があった。最後の葉であった。葉は枝の近くで濃い緑色をしていたが、葉の縁は黄色に変わりつつあった。葉は、地面から20フィートほどのところにぶら下がっていた。

　「最後の葉ね」ジョンジーは言った。「きっと夜のうちに散るだろうと思っていたわ。風の音が聞こえたもの。今日のうちに散って、同じ時にわたしも死ぬわ」

"Dear, dear Johnsy!" said Sue. "Think of me, if you won't think of yourself. What would I do?"

But Johnsy did not answer. The most lonely thing in the world is a soul when it is preparing to go on its far journey. The ties that held her to friendship and to earth were breaking, one by one.

The day slowly passed. As it grew dark, they could still see the leaf hanging from its branch against the wall. And then, as the night came, the north wind began again to blow. The rain still beat against the windows.

When it was light enough the next morning, Johnsy again commanded that she be allowed to see.

The leaf was still there.

Johnsy lay for a long time looking at it. And then she called to Sue, who was cooking something for her to eat.

"I've been a bad girl, Sue," said Johnsy. "Something has made that last leaf stay there to show me how bad I was. It is wrong to want to die. I'll try to eat now. But first bring me a looking-glass, so that I can see myself. And then I'll sit up and watch you cook."

■one by one 1つずつ　■be allowed to ～することを許される　■make A do Aに ～させる　■how ～ A was いかにAが～だったか　■It is wrong to ～. ～するのは間 違っている。

「ねえ、ジョンジー！ 自分のことを考えるつもりがないなら、わたしのことを考えて。わたしはどうしたらいいの？」

　だが、ジョンジーは答えなかった。この世で一番孤独なものは、遠い旅に発とうとしている魂である。友情や現世と彼女を結びつけていた絆は、一つずつ切れようとしていた。

　その日はゆっくりと過ぎていった。暗くなっても、壁を面した枝にぶらさがっている葉を見ることができた。それから夜が来た。ふたたび北風が吹き始めた。そのうえ雨も窓に打ち付けた。

　翌朝、明くなると、また、ジョンジーは、葉を見せてとスーに命じるように言った。

　葉は、まだ同じ場所にあった。

　ジョンジーは長い間、その葉を見つめていた。それから、彼女の食事を用意しているスーに声をかけた。

　「わたしって悪い子だったわ、スー。何かが、あの最後の葉をあそこに残しているのね。わたしがどんなに間違っていたかを教えるためにね。死にたいなんて思うのは間違っているのね。食べてみるわ。だけどそのまえに、自分を見たいから、鏡を持ってきて。ベッドに起きて、スーが料理をするのを見ているわ」

An hour later she said, "Sue, some day I hope to paint the Bay of Naples."

The doctor came in the afternoon. Sue followed him into the hall outside Johnsy's room to talk to him.

"The chances are good," said the doctor. He took Sue's thin, shaking hand in his. "Give her good care, and she'll get well. And now I must see another sick person in this house. His name is Behrman. A painter, I believe. Pneumonia, too. He is an old, weak man, and he is very ill. There is no hope for him. But we take him to the hospital today. We'll make it as easy for him as we can."

The next day the doctor said to Sue: "She's safe. You have done it. Food and care now——that's all."

And that afternoon Sue came to the bed where Johnsy lay. She put one arm around her.

"I have something to tell you," she said. "Mr. Behrman died of pneumonia today in the hospital. He was ill only two days. Someone found him on the morning of the first day, in his room. He was helpless with pain.

■take one's hand 手を取る、握る　■give ~ care ~の世話をする　■make it easy for A Aを楽にさせる　■You have done it. よくやった。成功だ。　■That's all. 以上です。それだけです。

1時間が過ぎたころ、「スー、いつかナポリ湾の絵を描きたいわ」と
ジョンジーが言った。

　午後、医者が往診に来た。医者と話すために、スーは医者のあとか
ら、ジョンジーの部屋の外の廊下に出た。

　「良くなる見込みは十分にある」。医者はそう言って、スーのほっそり
とした、ふるえる手を握った。「しっかり看病してやりなさい。そうす
れば彼女は元気になるよ。これから、この建物に住む病人をもう一人診
なければならない。バーマンという人だ。画家だと思うがね。彼も肺炎
だよ。老人で弱っていて、ひどく悪い。彼はまず快復の望みはない。だ
が、今日、病院へ運ぶことにしている。できるだけ彼を楽にしてあげた
いと思っているよ」

　翌日、医者はスーに言った。「ジョンジーはもう大丈夫だ。よくやっ
たね。今必要なのは食べ物と世話、それだけだよ」

　そして、その日の午後、スーはジョンジーのベッドのところに行き
ジョンジーを片手で抱いた。

　「言わなければならないことあるの」とスーは言った。「バーマンさん
が、肺炎で病院で亡くなったの。病気だったのはたった2日間。最初の
日の朝、誰かが部屋でバーマンさんを見つけたの。苦痛で手のほどこし
ようのない状態だった。

"His shoes and his clothes were wet and as cold as ice. Everyone wondered where he had been. The night had been so cold and wild.

"And then they found some things. There was a light that he had taken outside. And there were his materials for painting. There was paint, green paint and yellow paint. And——

"Look out the window, dear, at the last leaf on the wall. Didn't you wonder why it never moved when the wind was blowing? Oh, my dear, it is Behrman's great masterpiece——he painted it there the night that the last leaf fell."

■as ～ as … まるで…のように～だ　■wonder 動 ～かしらと不思議に思う　■wild 形 大荒れの

靴と服は濡れていて、氷のように冷たかった。誰もがバーマンさんが
どこにいたのか不思議に思ったわ。その夜は、ひどく寒くて、荒れた天
気だったから。

　いくつか見つかった物があるの。バーマンさんが外に持ち出したライ
ト。画材。そしてグリーンと黄色の絵の具があったの。それから──。

　窓の外の壁の最後に残った葉を見て。風が吹いても、葉が絶対に動か
ないことを不思議に思わなかった？　ねえ、ジョンジー、あの葉はバー
マンさんの最高傑作よ。最後の葉が散った夜、バーマンさんがあの葉を
あの場所に描いたのよ」

覚えておきたい英語表現

　この作品は、ジョンジーの生きる力を支えるために自らの命を犠牲に
した画家バーマンの自己犠牲の精神を描いた物語です。描かれたのは
ツタ（ivy）の葉ですが、日本の俳句にも「桐一葉」という秋の季語があ
りますね。初秋に桐の一葉が散る a falling leaf from a paulownia 風景
を滅びの兆し the beginning of the end として詠うわけです。落葉に自
分の命の終わりを重ねるジョンジーのせつない心境がよく理解できる
からこそ本作品が日本で広く読まれ続けているのでしょう。

Suppose a painter had some painting materials for which he had
not paid. Suppose he had no money. Suppose a man came to get
the money.（p.38, 5-7行目）
ある画家が画材をいくらか手に入れて、その支払いが済んでいなかったとしたら
どうだろう。彼が金を持っていなかったとしたらどうだろう。ある男がその代金
を取り立てにやって来たとしたらどうだろう。

【解説】Suppose ~ の「もし~ならばどうだろう」という命令法の用法が3文つづい
ています。Supposeの後にはthatが省略されています。このthat節は仮定法にな
っていることに注意しましょう。

> She lay on her bed almost without moving. （p.40, 下から4行目）
> 彼女はほとんど身動きもせずベッドに横たわっていた。

【解説】ここでは、自動詞lie「横たわる」の過去形layが使われていますが、これと他動詞lay「〜を横たえる」を混同しないように注意しましょう。
自動詞lieの活用形はlie-lay-lain、他動詞layの活用形はlay-laid-laidとなることも覚えておきましょう。

（他動詞layの例文）
She laid her bag on the sofa.　彼女はバッグをソファーの上に置いた。

> When the last one falls, I must go, too. （p.44, 下から2-1行目）
> 最後の葉が落ちるとき、わたしも死ぬのね。

【解説】「死ぬ」には、dieとかpass away, leave this worldなど様々な表現がありますが、goという表現には苦い思い出があります。
ニューヨークに赴任して間もないころのこと。先に帰宅してしまったアメリカ人のアシスタントに電話がかかってきたのです。他に人もおらず、おそるおそる電話を取った私は、She has already gone. と言ってしまったのです。相手は、大声でWhat?　と叫ぶように聞き返しました。その反応で私は、「彼女なら死んでしまったよ」と言ってしまったことに気づいて、She has already gone home.（彼女なら帰宅しました）と言い直したものの、冷や汗をかいてしまいました。goを使うときはくれぐれもご用心を。

What does an old tree have to do with you? （p.46, 2-3行目）
あなたと老木はどういう関係があるの？

【解説】このhave toはもちろんmustの意味ではなく、have to do with ～で「～
と関係がある」という意味になります。
次の語句も一緒に覚えておきましょう。

have something to do with ～　　～と少し関係がある

have nothing to do with ～　　～とまったく関係がない

have little to do with ～　　～とほとんど関係がない

The Cop and the Anthem

警官と賛美歌

oapy moved restlessly on his seat in Madison Square. There are certain signs to show that winter is coming. Birds begin to fly south. Women who want nice new warm coats become very kind to their husbands. And Soapy moves restlessly on his seat in the park. When you see these signs, you know that winter is near.

A dead leaf fell at Soapy's feet. That was a special sign for him that winter was coming. It was time for all who lived in Madison Square to prepare.

Soapy's mind now realized the fact. The time had come. He had to find some way to take care of himself during the cold weather. And therefore he moved restlessly on his seat.

■certain 形 若干の、わずかの　■show that ～ということを示す　■It is time for A to ～. Aが～する時間だ。　■all who live in ～に住むすべての者　■take care of oneself 自分の身を守る

ソーピイは、マジソン・スクエアのいつもの自分の場所で、落ち着きがなかった。冬が間近いということを示す兆候がいくつかある。鳥は南へ向かい始めている。素敵な、新しくて暖かいコートが欲しいご婦人たちは、夫に対してとても親切になっている。そしてソーピイは、公園の定位置で、落ち着きがない。こういう兆候が現れると、冬が間近いのだ。

　枯れ葉が1枚、ソーピイの足元に落ちてきた。これは、ソーピイにとって、冬が近いという特別の徴(しるし)なのだ。マジソン・スクエアで暮らす者たちが、準備をしなければならない時が来たのだ。

　ソーピイは、今やその事実を認識していた。時が来たのだ。寒い冬のあいだ、身を処すすべを見つけなければならない。それで、自分のいつもの場所で落ち着かないのだ。

Soapy's hopes for the winter were not very high. He was not thinking of sailing away on a ship. He was not thinking of southern skies, or of the Bay of Naples. Three months in the prison on Blackwell's Island was what he wanted. Three months of food every day and a bed every night, three months safe from the cold north wind and safe from cops. This seemed to Soapy the most desirable thing in the world.

For years, Blackwell's Island had been his winter home. Richer New Yorkers made their large plans to go to Florida or to the shore of the Mediterranean Sea each winter. Soapy made his small plans for going to the Island.

And now the time had come. Three big newspapers, some under his coat and some over his legs, had not kept him warm during the night in the park. So Soapy was thinking of the Island.

There were places in the city where he could go and ask for food and a bed. These would be given to him. He could move from one building to another, and he would be taken care of through the winter. But he liked Blackwell's Island better.

■think of ～のことを考える、検討する　■sail away 船出する　■Blackwell's Island ブラックウェルズ島《→p.87》　■seem to ～のように見える、思える　■for years 何年も、長期にわたり　■keep ～ warm ～を保温する　■ask for ～を求める

ソーピイは、冬のことでそれほど高望みをしているわけではなかった。船で航海に出るなんてことは考えていない。南の空も、ナポリ湾のことも頭にない。彼の望みは、ブラックウェルズ島の刑務所での3ヵ月なのだ。その3ヵ月間は、毎日、食事が保障され、毎夜、ベッドが与えられ、冷たい北風からも、警官からも守られる。ソーピイには、こういうことが世界で一番望ましいことのように思えるのだった。

　長年にわたり、ブラックウェルズ島はソーピイの冬の家だった。金持ちのニューヨーカーたちは、フロリダや地中海の海岸へ出かける大計画を立てていた。ソーピイは島へ行くというささやかな計画を立てたのだ。

　そして今、その時は来ていた。3枚の大きな新聞紙は、その数枚をコートの下に入れ、数枚で脚をくるんでいたが、公園の夜の寒さから彼を守ってくれてはいなかった。そこで、ソーピイは島へ行くことを考えているのだ。

　ニューヨークには、食べ物とベッドを頼めば、提供してくれるところが何ヵ所かあった。そこでは食べ物もベッドもソーピイに与えられる。冬の間、そういった場所を移動して、面倒をみてもらうこともできるだろう。だが、ソーピイはブラックウェルズ島のほうが気に入っていた。

Soapy's spirit was proud. If he went to any of these places, there were certain things he had to do. In one way or another, he would have to pay for what they gave him. They would not ask him for money. But they would make him wash his whole body. They would make him answer questions; they would want to know everything about his life.

No. Prison was better than that. The prison had rules that he would have to follow. But in prison a gentleman's own life was still his own life.

Soapy, having decided to go to the Island, at once began to move toward his desire.

There were many easy ways of doing this. The most pleasant way was to go and have a good dinner at some fine restaurant. Then he would say that he had no money to pay. And then a cop would be called. It would all be done very quietly. The cop would arrest him. He would be taken to a judge. The judge would do the rest.

■in one way or another あれこれと　■pay for ～の対価を払う　■at once すぐに
■move toward ～に近づく　■fine restaurant 高級レストラン　■be taken to ～に
連れて行かれる　■do the rest 残りのことをやる

ソーピイは、誇り高い精神の持ち主だった。こういった場所に行く
と、しなければならないことがあるのだ。あれこれ、提供されるものに
対して対価を支払わなければならなかった。そこにいる人たちが、金を
要求するわけではない。そのかわり、ソーピイに全身を洗わせ、いろい
ろな質問に答えさせ、彼の人生についてすべてを知ろうとするのだ。

　いや、刑務所はそれよりましだ。そこには従わなければならない規則
はある。だが、それでも、刑務所では紳士の人生は紳士自身のものなの
だ。
　ソーピイは、島に行くことを決めると、すぐに望みを達成すべく行動
を起こした。
　望みを達成するには、簡単な方法がいろいろある。もっとも好もしい
のは、素晴らしいレストランに行ってうまいディナーをとることだ。そ
のあと、金を持っていないんです、と言う。すると警官が呼ばれるだろ
う。すべてのことがとても静かに行われる。警官は彼を逮捕するだろ
う。彼は判事のもとへ送られる。あとは判事の仕事だ。

Soapy left his seat and walked slowly out of Madison Square to the place where the great street called Broadway and Fifth Avenue meet. He went across this wide space and started north on Broadway. He stopped at a large and brightly lighted restaurant. This was where the best food and the best people in the best clothes appeared every evening.

Soapy believed that above his legs he looked all right. His face was clean. His coat was good enough. If he could get to a table, he believed that success would be his. The part of him that would be seen above the table would look all right. The waiter would bring him what he asked for.

He began thinking of what he would like to eat. In his mind he could see the whole dinner. The cost would not be too high. He did not want the restaurant people to feel any real anger. But the dinner would leave him filled and happy for the journey to his winter home.

But as Soapy put his foot inside the restaurant door, the head waiter saw his broken old shoes and the torn clothes that covered his legs. Strong and ready hands turned Soapy around and moved him quietly and quickly outside again.

■go across 横断する　■get to a table テーブルに着く　■his 代 彼のもの　■would like to ～したい　■want A to ～ Aに～してほしい　■leave A ～ Aを～のままにする　■turn ～ around ～を方向転換させる

ソーピイは自分の居場所を離れ、マディソン・スクエアを出て、ブロードウェイと呼ばれる大通りと五番街が交わる地点へ向かった。その広い場所を横切って、ブロードウェイを北に向かって歩き始めた。大きな、煌々と明かりのついたレストランのところで立ち止まった。ここには、毎晩、最高の食べ物があり、最上の服に身を包んだ最高の人々が姿を見せた。

　ソーピイは脚から上については、問題がないと思った。顔は汚れてないし、上着も十分見られる。テーブルに着くことができたら、成功したも同然だと思った。テーブルの上から出ている部分については、問題はない。ウェイターは注文した料理を運んできてくれるだろう。

　彼は、何を食べたいのか考え始めた。彼は頭の中にディナーのすべてを思い描くことができた。それほど高くはないだろう。ソーピイは、レストランの人たちを本気で怒らせたくはなかったが、そのディナーは、冬の家へ向かう旅路の間、彼に満足感と幸福感を残してくれるはずだ。

　ところが、ソーピイがレストランのドアの内側に足を踏み入れるなり、ウェイター頭はソーピイの破れた古靴と脚を覆っている裂けた服に気がついた。屈強で断固とした手は、ソーピイに有無を言わせず方向転換させ、あっという間に外へ押し出した。

Soapy turned off Broadway. It seemed that this easy, this most desirable, way to the Island was not to be his. He must think of some other way of getting there.

At a corner of Sixth Avenue was a shop with a wide glass window, bright with electric lights. Soapy picked up a big stone and threw it through the glass. People came running around the corner. A cop was the first among them. Soapy stood still, and he smiled when he saw the cop.

"Where's the man that did that?" asked the cop.

"Don't you think that I might have done it?" said Soapy. He was friendly and happy. What he wanted was coming toward him.

But the cop's mind would not consider Soapy. Men who break windows do not stop there to talk to cops. They run away as fast as they can. The cop saw a man further along the street, running. He ran after him. And Soapy, sick at heart, walked slowly away. He had failed two times.

■turn off ～の関心をなくす　■It seems that ～ . ～のようだ。　■might have ～したかもしれない　■run away 逃げる、走り去る　■further along the street 通りのもっと先に　■sick at heart がっかりして

ソーピーはブロードウェイをあきらめた。島へ行くのに一番簡単で好ましい、この方法は彼に向いていなかった。そこへ行くために他の方法を考えなければならなかった。

　六番街の角に、大きなガラス窓がある店があった。窓は電気の光で明るく照らされていた。ソーピイは大きな石を拾い上げ、ガラスに向かって投げつけた。人々が角のあたりへ走って来た。真っ先にやって来たのは警官だった。ソーピイはじっと立っていた。そして、警官を見て、にっと笑った。

　「こんなことしたヤツはどこだ？」警官が言った。

　「おれがやったかもしれないと思わないのかい？」ソーピイは言った。彼は友好的で、幸せな気分であった。望んでいたものが、彼に近づいてきたのだ。

　だが、警官はソーピイのことなど考えてもいなかったようだ。窓を壊すような男たちは、警官と話すためにその場に残ったりするはずがなく、さっさと逃げ去るはずだ。その警官は、通りのもっと先に走っていく男を見つけて、後を追った。ソーピイといえば、がっかりしてのろのろと歩き去った。二度も失敗したのだ。

Across the street was another restaurant. It was not so fine as the one on Broadway. The people who went there were not so rich. Its food was not so good. Into this, Soapy took his old shoes and his torn clothes, and no one stopped him. He sat down at a table and was soon eating a big dinner. When he had finished, he said that he and money were strangers.

"Get busy and call a cop," said Soapy. "And don't keep a gentleman waiting."

"No cop for you," said the waiter. He called another waiter.

The two waiters threw Soapy upon his left ear on the hard street outside. He stood up slowly, one part at a time, and beat the dust from his clothes. Prison seemed only a happy dream. The Island seemed very far away. A cop who was standing near laughed and walked away.

06

Soapy traveled almost half a mile before he tried again. This time he felt very certain that he would be successful. A nice-looking young woman was standing before a shop window looking at the objects inside. Very near stood a large cop.

■A and B are strangers. AとBとはご無沙汰である。縁がない。 ■get busy すぐに取り掛かる ■keep ~ waiting ~を待たせておく ■No ~ for you. あなたに~は必要ない。 ■through ~ upon ~を投げ出す ■one part at a time 1つずつ、ゆっくりと ■mile マイル《およそ1,609.34m》 ■feel certain that ~だという確信がある

通りの向こうに、もうひとつレストランがあった。ブロードウェイの
レストランほど素敵ではなかった。そこの客たちは、それほど金持ちで
はなく、料理もそれほどうまいというわけではなかった。ソーピイは古
靴と破れた服を身に着けたまま、このレストランへ入ったが、誰も彼
を押しとどめようとはしなかった。テーブルについて、すぐに盛大に夕
食を食べ始めた。食べ終わると、自分は金には縁がないのだが、と言っ
た。

「すぐ、警官を呼んでくれ。紳士を待たせるもんじゃないぜ」

「おまえには警官なんぞいらないよ」とウェイターは言って、別のウェ
イターを呼び、二人がかりでソーピイを外に放り出した。ソーピイは左
耳を固い道路でひどく打ち、やっとの思いでのろのろと立ち上がり、服
のほこりを払った。刑務所は、幸せな夢にすぎず、島はひどく遠のいて
しまったようだった。近くに立っていた警官は、笑って、行ってしまっ
た。

　ソーピイは半マイルほど行ったところで、もう一度試そうとした。今
回は、成功するという確信があった。見た目のいい若い女性が、ショー
ウィンドの前に立ち、中のものを眺めていた。そのすぐ近くに大男の警
官が立っていた。

Soapy's plan was to speak to the young woman. She seemed to be a very nice young lady, who would not want a strange man to speak to her. She would ask the cop for help. And then Soapy would be happy to feel the cop's hand on his arm. He would be on his way to the Island.

He went near her. He could see that the cop was already watching him. The young woman moved away a few steps. Soapy followed. Standing beside her he said:

"Good evening, Bedelia! Don't you want to come and play with me?"

The cop was still looking. The young woman had only to move her hand, and Soapy would be on his way to the place where he wanted to go. He was already thinking how warm he would be.

The young woman turned to him. Putting out her hand, she took his arm.

"Sure, Mike," she said joyfully. "If you'll buy me something to drink. I would have spoken to you sooner, but the cop was watching."

■seem to ～のように見える、思える　■ask A for ～　Aに～を求める　■on one's way to ～へ向かって進んで　■move one's hand 手を振る　■put out one's hand 手を差し出す　■Sure. はい。いいですよ。

ソーピイの計画では、その若い女性にまず話しかける。女性は、知らない男に話しかけられるのをよしとしない、非常に育ちのいいレディのように見えた。多分、彼女は警官に助けを求めるだろう。そうしたら、ソーピイは自分の腕をつかむ警官の手を感じて幸せになるだろう。島行きが待っているというわけだ。

　ソーピイはその女性に近づいた。警官が彼を見ているのに気がついていた。その若い女性は数歩歩いて、窓から離れた。ソーピイはその後を追い、彼女の脇に立って言った。

　「いい晩だな、ベデリア！　おれと遊ばないか？」

　警官がじっと見ていた。その女性が手を振りさえすれば、ソーピイは望みの場所に行くことになるのだ。これでどんなに暖かくなるのかと、先走って考えていた。

　女性は振り返り、手を差し伸べて彼の腕をとった。

　「いいわ、マイク」。女性は明るく言った。「何か飲み物を買ってもらえるならね。もっと早く話しかけたかったけど、でもおまわりが見ていたでしょ」

With the young woman holding his arm, Soapy walked past the cop. He was filled with sadness. He was still free. Was he going to remain free forever?

At the next corner he pulled his arm away and ran.

When he stopped, he was near several theaters. In this part of the city, streets are brighter and hearts are more joyful than in other parts. Women and men in rich, warm coats moved happily in the winter air.

A sudden fear caught Soapy. No cop was going to arrest him.

Then he came to another cop standing in front of a big theater. He thought of something else to try.

He began to shout as if he had had too much to drink. His voice was as loud as he could make it. He danced, he cried out.

And the cop turned his back to Soapy, and said to a man standing near him, "It's one of those college boys. He won't hurt anything. We had orders to let them shout."

Soapy was quiet. Was no cop going to touch him? He began to think of the Island as if it were as far away as Heaven. He pulled his thin coat around him. The wind was very cold.

■walk past ～とすれ違う ■man in a coat コートを着た男性 ■fear catch ～が恐怖にとらわれる ■as if あたかも～のように ■cry out 叫ぶ ■turn one's back to ～に背を向ける ■pull one's coat around コートの前をかき合せる

女性に腕をとられて、ソーピイは警官のそばを通り過ぎた。彼は、悲嘆にくれていた。彼は、まだ自由の身だ。永遠に自由のままなのだろうか?

　次の角で、腕を振りほどき、走った。

　立ち止まると、近くに劇場がいくつかあった。ニューヨークのこのあたりでは、通りはいっそう輝きを増し、気分は他の場所よりさらに浮き立った。ふんわりとした、暖かいコートを着た女性や男性が、満ち足りたようすで冬の空気のなかを行きかっていた。

　突然、恐怖がソーピイを襲った。どの警官も彼を逮捕しようとしなかった。

　それから、大きな劇場の前に立っている別の警官に出会った。彼は何か別のことをやろうと思いついた。

　そして、酒を飲み過ぎたかのように、大声で叫び出した。精一杯、大声を出し、踊り、叫んだ。

　警官はソーピイに背を向け、隣の男に言った。「ヤツはまあ学生で、何も傷つけたりはしませんよ。われわれは、学生たちが大声を出しても放っておくように、指示されていましてね」

　ソーピイは黙った。警官は、彼に触れようともしないのか?　いまや、島は天国ほど遠くへ行ってしまったように思えてきた。薄いコートを引っ張り上げた。風はひどく冷たかった。

Then he saw a man in a shop buying a newspaper. The man's umbrella stood beside the door. Soapy stepped inside the shop, took the umbrella and walked slowly away. The man followed him quickly.

"My umbrella," he said.

"Oh, is it?" said Soapy. "Why don't you call a cop? I took it. Your umbrella! Why don't you call a cop? There's one standing at the corner."

The man walked more slowly. Soapy did the same. But he had a feeling that he was going to fail again. The cop looked at the two men.

"I——" said the umbrella man "——that is——you know how these things happen——I——if that's your umbrella I'm very sorry——I found it this morning in a restaurant— if you say it's yours——I hope you'll——"

"It's mine!" cried Soapy with anger in his voice.

The umbrella man hurried away. The cop helped a lady across the street. Soapy walked east. He threw the umbrella as far as he could throw it. He talked to himself about cops and what he thought of them. Because he wished to be arrested, they seemed to believe he was like a king, who could do no wrong.

■Why don't you ～? ～したらどうだい？　■hurry away そそくさと立ち去る
■talk to oneself 独り言を言う　■do wrong 悪事を働く

それから、彼は店で新聞を買っている男を目にした。男の傘がドアの脇にて立てかけてあった。ソーピイは店に入り、傘を手にして、ゆっくりその場を離れた。男はすぐに後を追ってきた。

「ぼくの傘だよ」と、男は言った。

「えっ、そうかい？　なぜおまわりを呼ばないんだ？　おれはあんたの傘を盗んだんだぜ。おまわりを呼んだらいいんじゃないか？　あの角にひとり立っているぜ」

　男は、さらにゆっくりと近づいてきた。ソーピイも近づいた。だが、またもや失敗しそうだという予感がした。警官は二人の方を見た。

「ぼくは――」と傘の男が言った。「――ええっと、こういったことがどうして起こるかおわかりですよね。この傘が、あなたのものでしたら、すみませんでした。ええっと――今朝、レストランでこの傘を見つけたのです。あなたが、自分のものだと言われるのでしたらどうか――」

「おれの傘だ」ソーピイは怒って怒鳴った。

　傘の男は、急いで立ち去った。警官は、通りを渡る女性の手助けをしていた。ソーピイは東へ向かった。傘を思いっきり遠くへ投げ捨て、警官たちについて思いのたけをぶつぶつつぶやいた。逮捕されたいと思っているのに、警官たちは、ソーピイを、何ひとつ悪事をはたらかない、王様のような人間だと思っているふしがある。

At last Soapy came to one of the quiet streets on the east side of the city. He turned here and began to walk south toward Madison Square. He was going home, although home was only a seat in a park.

But on a very quiet corner Soapy stopped. Here was an old, old church. Through one colored-glass window came a soft light. Sweet music came to Soapy's ears and seemed to hold him there.

The moon was above, peaceful and bright. There were few people passing. He could hear birds high above him.

And the anthem that came from the church held Soapy there, for he had known it well long ago. In those days, his life contained such things as mothers, and flowers, and high hopes, and friends, and clean thoughts, and clean clothes.

Soapy's mind was ready for something like this. He had come to the old church at the right time. There was a sudden and wonderful change in his soul. He saw with sick fear how he had fallen. He saw his worthless days, his wrong desires, his dead hopes, the lost power of his mind.

■at last とうとう　■hold ~ there　~をそこに釘付けにする　■anthem 图 賛美歌
■for 暖 ~だから　■in those days あの頃は　■high hopes 野望　■be ready for ~
準備が整って

とうとうソーピイは街の東側の静かな通りへ来た。ここで向きを変え、マジソン・スクエアへ向けて南へ歩き始めた。彼は家へ帰る途中であった。家といっても、公園のベンチにすぎないのだが。

　だが、ひどく静かな角でソーピイは立ち止まった。そこには古い、古い教会があった。一枚の色ガラスの窓から、柔らかな光が流れ出ていた。心地よい音楽が、ソーピイの耳に届き、彼をそこに押しとどめるかのようだった。
　空には月が、穏やかに明るく輝いていた。道を行く人は、ほとんどいなかった。頭上では、鳥の声が聞こえていた。
　そして、教会から聞こえてくる讃美歌が、ソーピイをそこへ釘づけにしたのだ。というのも、それは、ずっと昔からよく知っている歌だった。あのころの彼の人生には、母親や花、高邁な望み、友人たち、真っ当な考え、清潔な衣類などがあった。
　ソーピイの心は、讃美歌のようなものを受け入れようとしていた。彼は、本当にいいときに古い教会に来たのであった。彼の心には、思いがけない、そして素晴らしい変化が生まれた。彼は自分がどのようにして堕ちていったかを省みて、吐き気をもよおすほどの恐怖を覚えた。自堕落な日々、間違った願望、失った希望　そして失くしてしまった精神力を省みた。

And, also, in a moment his heart answered this change in his soul. He would fight to change his life. He would pull himself up, out of the mud. He would make a man of himself again.

There was time. He was young enough. He would find his old purpose in life, and follow it. That sweet music had changed him. Tomorrow he would find work. A man had once offered him a job. He would find that man tomorrow. He would be somebody in the world. He would——

Soapy felt a hand on his arm. He looked quickly around into the broad face of a cop. "What are you doing hanging around here?" asked the cop.

"Nothing," said Soapy.

"You think I believe that?" said the cop.

Full of his new strength, Soapy began to argue. And it is not wise to argue with a New York cop.

"Come along," said the cop.

"Three months on the Island," said the Judge to Soapy the next morning.

■fight to ～のために闘う ■pull oneself up 自分を引き上げる ■hang around う
ろつく ■Come along. さあ来なさい。

そして一瞬、彼の心はこの変化に応えたのだ。人生を変えるために闘おう。汚泥の中から抜け出そう。再び、自分を男にしよう。

　その時が来たのだ。彼はまだ若い。かつての自分が人生に持っていた目的を見出して、それに従っていこう。あの、心地よい音楽が彼を変えたのだ。明日、仕事を見つけよう。以前、仕事を提供してくれた人がいた。明日、その人に会いに行こう。世間で、ひとかどの人間になろう。そうなろう──。

　ソーピイは自分の腕に手が置かれたことに気付いた。振り返ると、警官の大きな顔がそこにあった。「このあたりをなんでうろついているんだ?」と警官が尋ねた。

　「べつに」ソーピイは答えた。

　「おれが、そんなことを信じるとでも思っているのか?」

　新しい力を得て、ソーピイは口論を始めた。だが、ニューヨークの警官と口論をするのは、賢明ではない。

　「ちょっと来い」警官は言った。

　「島へ3ヵ月」判事が翌朝ソーピイに言い渡した。

覚えておきたい英語表現

　マンハッタンの公園で暮らすhomelessのソーピイは、寒い冬を控えて収容施設shelterに入るよりはと、わざと罪を犯して刑務所で3ヵ月を過ごそうとします。ところが、警官copも周囲も彼の行為をとがめない。落胆してねぐらに戻ろうとしたソーピイは偶然耳にした賛美歌に改心し、人生をやり直そうとします。その瞬間、警官に見とがめられ、翌朝、ブラックウェルズ島の刑務所行きという判決が言い渡されてしまうのです。聖から俗へ、俗から聖へと揺れ動くソーピイの心を警官copと讃美歌anthemの対比の中に描き、かつ人生の皮肉という普遍的なテーマをも感じさせる掌編ですね。anthemは、われわれにはなじみが薄かった単語ですが、スポーツの国際試合で国歌national anthemを耳にすることも多くなりました。

> It was time for all who lived in Madison Square to prepare.
> （p.64, 下から5-4行目）
> マジソン・スクエアで暮らす者たちが、準備をしなければならない時が来たのだ。

【解説】it is time for ＋人＋ to do「（人）が～すべき時間」は、よく使われる表現です。これとよく似た言い回しに、仮定法を用いる場合があります。
it is (high) time (that) ～「もう当然～していい時間である」という表現で、このthat節内の動詞は仮定法過去で表されます。

　　　It's time (that) kids went to bed.　もう子どもは寝る時間だよ。

> Soapy turned off Broadway. (p.72, 1行目)
> ソーピーはブロードウェイをあきらめた。

【解説】turn offは、たとえばDon't forget to turn the light off.（明りを消すことを忘れないようにね）というように、「スイッチを切る」「栓を締める」という意味で使われることが多いのですが、ここでは「～への関心をなくす」という意味で使われています。

> When he had finished, he said that he and money were strangers.
> (p.74, 5-6行目)
> 食べ終わると、自分は金には縁がないのだが、と言った。

【解説】strangerは他人、よその人という意味です。この文章はつまり、お金を擬人化していて、ソーピーはマネー君を知らない、関係ない、縁がないとなるわけです。

Blackwell's Island　ブラックウェルズ島 (p.66, 4行目)

ニューヨークの中心マンハッタン島とクイーンズ区の間を流れるイーストリバーに浮かぶ島。現在はRoosevelt Island（ルーズベルト島）と呼ばれています。1828年まではブラックウェル家が所有していたので、この名が付いていたのです。そこに刑務所があったのですね。私の先輩駐在員はこの島に住んでいました。もちろん刑務所にではありませんが。ただし、ご本人はケンカをして留置所に一晩お世話になったことはあるそうです。O.Henry自身も横領の罪で3年ほど服役して作品を書きましたから、作家にとってはあながち悪い事ばかりでもないのかも知れませんね……。

A Retrieved Reformation

改心

07

In the prison shoe shop, Jimmy Valentine was busily at work making shoes. A prison officer came into the shop and led Jimmy to the prison office. There Jimmy was given an important paper. It said that he was free.

Jimmy took the paper without showing much pleasure or interest. He had been sent to prison to stay for four years. He had been there for ten months. But he had expected to stay only three months. Jimmy Valentine had many friends outside the prison. A man with so many friends does not expect to stay in prison long.

"Valentine," said the chief prison officer, "you'll go out tomorrow morning. This is your chance. Make a man of yourself. You're not a bad fellow at heart. Stop breaking safes open, and live a better life."

■at work 仕事中で　■It say that ～. それによると～だと（書いて）ある。　■chief 图
所長　■make a man of ～を一人前の男にする　■at heart 本質的には　■breaking
safes open 金庫破りをすること

ジミー・ヴァレンタインは、刑務所の靴屋で、忙しく靴作りをしていた。刑務官が店に来て、ジミーを事務所に連れて行った。そこで、ジミーは重要な書類をもらった。それには、釈放とあった。

　ジミーは、それほどの喜びも関心も見せずに、その書類を手にとった。彼は、懲役4年の刑で、刑務所に送られたのだった。すでに10ヵ月をここで過ごしていた。だが、彼は、刑務所にいるのは3ヵ月だけ、と思っていたのだ。ジミー・ヴァレンタインは刑務所の外に友だちが沢山いた。友だちがとても多い男は、刑務所に長滞在するだろうとは思わない。
　「ヴァレンタイン。おまえは明朝、釈放される。またとない機会だ。立派な男になるんだな。おまえは根っからの悪人ではない。金庫破りはやめて、もっとましな人生を送るように」刑務官長は言った。

"Me?" said Jimmy in surprise. "I never broke open a safe in my life."

"Oh, no," the chief prison officer laughed. "Never. Let's see. How did you happen to get sent to prison for opening that safe in Springfield? Was it because you didn't want to tell where you really were? Perhaps because you were with some lady, and you didn't want to tell her name? Or was it because the judge didn't like you? You men always have a reason like that. You never go to prison because you broke open a safe."

"Me?" Jimmy said. His face still showed surprise. "I was never in Springfield in my life."

"Take him away," said the chief prison officer. "Get him the clothes he needs for going outside. Bring him here again at seven in the morning. And think about what I said, Valentine."

At a quarter past seven on the next morning, Jimmy stood again in the office. He had on some new clothes that did not fit him, and a pair of new shoes that hurt his feet. These are the usual clothes given to a prisoner when he leaves the prison.

■break open こじ開ける　■safe 图 金庫　■Let's see. さてと。どれどれ。　■happen to 期せずして〜する　■you men お前たち男ども　■get A something Aに〜を与える　■a quarter past 〜時15分

「おれがですか?」ジミーは驚いて言った。「これまで、金庫破りなん
ぞ、ただの一度もしたことはありませんよ」

「まさか」刑務官長は笑い出した。「ただの一度もか。さてと。どのよ
うな理由でスプリングフィールドの金庫破りの件で、刑務所に送られる
はめになったのかね。おまえが本当はどこにいたのかを話したくなかっ
たからなのかね。おそらく女と一緒で、女の名前を言いたくなかったか
らではないのかな。それとも、判事に嫌われたせいなのか。男には、い
つもそういった理由があるものだ。おまえは決して金庫破りをしたから
ではないと言うのだな」

「おれがですか?」いまだに驚いたようすで、ジミーが言った。「スプ
リングフィールドになんか行ったことなどないですよ」

「こいつを連れて行け。出所するのに必要な衣類をやってくれ。明朝
7時にまた、ここへ連れてきてくれ。それからわしが言ったことをよく
考えておけよ、ヴァレンタイン」と刑務官長は言った。

翌朝、7時15分にジミーはふたたび事務室に立っていた。ちっとも
合っていない新品の服を着て、新品の靴が彼の足を傷めていた。こう
いったものは、受刑者が出所する際に供与される通常の衣類であった。

Next they gave him money to pay for his trip on a train to the city near the prison. They gave him five dollars more. The five dollars were supposed to help him become a better man.

Then the chief prison officer put out his hand for a handshake. That was the end of Valentine, Prisoner 9762. Mr. James Valentine walked out into the sunshine.

He did not listen to the song of the birds or look at the green trees or smell the flowers. He went straight to a restaurant. There he tasted the first sweet joys of being free. He had a good dinner. After that he went to the train station. He gave some money to a blind man who sat there asking for money, and then he got on the train.

Three hours later he got off the train in a small town. Here he went to the restaurant of Mike Dolan.

Mike Dolan was alone there. After shaking hands he said, "I'm sorry we couldn't do it sooner, Jimmy my boy. But there was that safe in Springfield, too. It wasn't easy. Feeling all right?"

"Fine," said Jimmy. "Is my room waiting for me?"

■be supposed to do 〜することになっている　■put out one's hand 手を差し出す
■ask for money 施しを求める　■get on 〜に乗る　■get off 〜から降りる　■my boy 君、ほら《親しみをこめた呼びかけ》

つぎに、刑務所から近くの町まで汽車に乗って行くための金が与えられた。それから、さらにもう5ドルが与えられた。この金は、ジミーがもっとましな人間になるのに役立てられるはずであった。

　それから刑務官長は、握手のために手を差し出した。これで、受刑者9762号ヴァレンタインはいなくなったのだ。ジェームズ・ヴァレンタイン氏は、陽光に向かって歩き出した。

　彼は、鳥のさえずりに耳を傾けようともせず、みどりの木々に目もくれず、花の香りをかごうともせずに、まっすぐレストランに向かった。レストランで、はじめて自由の身である爽快な喜びを味わい、結構な夕食をとった。その後、駅へ向かった。駅では、座って施しを求めている目の不自由な男にいくばくかの金をやり、それから汽車に乗った。

　3時間後、小さな町で汽車から降り、マイク・ドーランのレストランへ行った。

　マイク・ドーランはレストランに一人でいた。握手をしてからマイクは言った。「早くこうできなかったのはすまなかった、ジミー。そうはいっても、スプリングフィールドの例の金庫の件もあったしな。だから簡単ではなかったんだ。気分はどうだい」

　「上々さ。おれの部屋は大丈夫かい?」

He went up and opened the door of a room at the back of the house. Everything was as he had left it. It was here they had found Jimmy, when they took him to prison. There on the door was a small piece of cloth. It had been torn from the coat of the cop, as Jimmy was fighting to escape.

There was a bed against the wall. Jimmy pulled the bed toward the middle of the room. The wall behind it looked like any wall, but now Jimmy found and opened a small door in it. From this opening he pulled out a dust-covered bag.

He opened this and looked lovingly at the tools for breaking open a safe. No finer tools could be found any place. They were complete; everything needed was here. They had been made of a special material, in the necessary sizes and shapes. Jimmy had planned them himself, and he was very proud of them.

It had cost him over nine hundred dollars to have these tools made at——, a place where they make such things for men who work at the job of safe-breaking.

■at the back of ～の奥に　■look like any ～ 何の変哲もない～のように見える　■be proud of ～を自慢に思う

2階へ上がり、奥の部屋のドアを開けた。すべてが、ジミーがここを離れたときのままであった。ジミーはここで警官たちに見つかり、刑務所に送られた。ドアの所には、小さな布切れが残っていた。ジミーが逃げようと警官ともみ合ったときに、警官のコートから千切れたものだった。

　壁に向けてベッドが置かれていた。ジミーは部屋の真ん中へベッドを引っ張った。ベッドの後ろはなんら変哲もない壁に見えたが、彼は、その壁に小さな扉をさがしだして開けた。その開け口から、ほこりだらけのバッグを引っ張りだした。

　彼はバッグを開けて、金庫破りの道具一式を愛おしげに眺めた。これ以上の道具はどこにも見当たらない。完全な一そろいで、必要なものすべてがここにあった。これらは、特別の材料で、必要な大きさと形状に作られていた。ジミーが自分で考案したのだ。そして、彼はこれらの道具を非常に自慢にしていた。

　こういった道具を作ってもらうのに、金庫破り御用達のところで、ジミーは900ドル以上も支払ったのだった。

In half an hour Jimmy went downstairs and through the restaurant. He was now dressed in good clothes that fitted him well. He carried his dusted and cleaned bag.

"Do you have anything planned?" asked Mike Dolan.

"Me?" asked Jimmy as if surprised. "I don't understand. I work for the New York Famous Bread and Cake Makers Company. And I sell the best bread and cake in the country."

Mike enjoyed these words so much that Jimmy had to take a drink with him. Jimmy had some milk. He never drank anything stronger.

A week after Valentine, 9762, left the prison, a safe was broken open in Richmond, Indiana. No one knew who did it. Eight hundred dollars were taken.

Two weeks after that, a safe in Logansport was opencd. It was a new kind of safe; it had been made, they said, so strong that no one could break it open. But someone did, and took fifteen hundred dollars.

■dress in ～を身につける ■fit ～ well ～にぴったり合う ■as if あたかも～のように ■so ～ that 非常に～なので… ■they say （噂で聞いたところによると）～らしい

30分後、階下へ降りて行き、レストランを通り抜けた。すでに、彼によく合った上等の服に着替え、ほこりを払ってきれいになったバッグを持ってきた。

　「何か計画があるのかね?」マイク・ドーランが尋ねた。

　「わたしがですか?」ジミーは、びっくりしたような様子で聞き返した。「何のことだかわかりませんね。ニューヨーク・フェーマス製菓会社に勤めているんです。この国で最高のパンと菓子を販売しています」

　マイクはジミーのことばをひどく面白がり、ジミーは彼と一杯飲むはめになった。ジミーはミルクを飲んだ。彼が強い飲み物を飲むことは決してなかった。

　ヴァレンタイン9762号が出所してから1週間もすると、インディアナ州リッチモンドで金庫が破られた。誰の仕業か誰にもわからなかった。盗られたのは800ドルだった。

　それから2週間後、ローガンスポートで金庫がこじ開けられた。それは新しいタイプの金庫であった。非常に頑丈にできているので、誰も破れないと評判の金庫だったが、誰かがこじ開け、1500ドルを盗んだのだ。

Then a safe in Jefferson City was opened. Five thousand dollars were taken. This loss was a big one. Ben Price was a cop who worked on such important matters, and now he began to work on this.

08

He went to Richmond, Indiana, and to Logansport, to see how the safe-breaking had been done in those places. He was heard to say:

"I can see that Jim Valentine has been here. He is in business again. Look at the way he opened this one. Everything easy, everything clean. He is the only man who has the tools to do it. And he is the only man who knows how to use tools like this. Yes, I want Mr. Valentine. Next time he goes to prison, he's going to stay there until his time is finished."

Ben Price knew how Jimmy worked. Jimmy would go from one city to another far away. He always worked alone. He always left quickly when he was finished. He enjoyed being with nice people. For all these reasons, it was not easy to catch Mr. Valentine.

People with safes full of money were glad to hear that Ben Price was at work trying to catch Mr. Valentine.

■He was heard to say: 彼から次の言葉が聞かれた　■I can see that ～. ～が分かります。　■in business 仕事中で　■until his time is finished 彼が死ぬまで　■It is not easy to ～. ～するのは容易ではない。

それからジェファーソン市でも金庫が破られ、5000ドルが盗られた。ここの被害額は大きかった。ベン・プライスはこういった重要事件を担当する刑事で、事件の捜査に乗り出した。

　彼は、インディアナ州のリッチモンドとローガンスポートへ出向き、その地で金庫破りがどうのように行われたのかを調べ、こう言ったのだ。

　「ジム・ヴァレンタインはここにいたな。ヤツはまた仕事を始めている。ヤツのこの金庫の開け方を見てみろよ。すべてが簡単に、そしてすっきりと行われている。こういう仕事ができる道具を持っている人間はヤツだけだ。そういった道具を使いこなせるのもヤツだけだ。そうさ、おれはヤツを追っているんだ。こんど刑務所に入ったら、死ぬまでそこにいることになるだろうよ」

　ベンはジミーの仕事の仕方を知っていた。ジミーは一つの町から、遠く離れた町へ移動するのだ。いつも一人で仕事をした。そして、仕事が終わると、素早く立ち去るのだった。愉快な人たちと一緒に過ごすのが好きだった。こういった理由で、ヴァレンタイン氏を捕えるのは容易なことではなかった。

　札束でいっぱいの金庫を持つ者たちは、ベン・プライスがヴァレンタイン氏をとらえる担当についたことを聞き、たいそう喜んだ。

One afternoon Jimmy Valentine and his bag arrived in a small town named Elmore. Jimmy, looking as young as a college boy, walked down the street toward the hotel.

A young lady walked across the street, passed him at the corner and entered a door. Over the door was the sign, "The Elmore Bank." Jimmy Valentine looked into her eyes, forgetting at once what he was. He became another man. She looked away, and brighter color came into her face. Young men like Jimmy did not appear often in Elmore.

Jimmy saw a boy near the bank door, and began to ask questions about the town. After a time the young lady came out and went on her way. She seemed not to see Jimmy as she passed him.

"Isn't that young lady Polly Simpson?" asked Jimmy.

"No," said the boy. "She's Annabel Adams. Her father owns this bank."

Jimmy went to the hotel, where he said his name was Ralph D. Spencer. He got a room there. He told the hotel man he had come to Elmore to go into business. How was the shoe business? Was there already a good shoe shop?

■sign 图 看板　■look away　視線をそらす　■after a time　しばらくして　■go on one's way　帰途に着く　■go into business　事業を始める

ある日の昼下がり、ジミー・ヴァレンタインと彼のバッグがエルモアという小さな町に到着した。ジミーは、ホテルに向かって通りを歩いて行った。彼の様子は学生のように若々しかった。

　若い女性が一人、通りを横切り、角でジミーを追い越し、ドアの中へ入ろうとしていた。ドアの上には「エルモア銀行」の看板があった。ジミー・ヴァレンタインは、彼女の目を見つめたその瞬間に自分が何者かを忘れた。彼は別の男になったのだ。彼女は目をそらして、顔を赤らめた。エルモアでは、ジミーのような若い男にそうそうお目にかかれるものではなかった。

　ジミーはドアの近くにいた少年に、町についていろいろ質問をし始めた。しばらくしてその令嬢が現れて、帰り道についた。彼女はジミーのそばを通り過ぎるとき、彼を見てはいないようだった。

　「あの令嬢は、ポリー・シンプソンではないよね」ジミーは尋ねた。
　「ええ、アナベル・アダムズさんです。お父さんが、この銀行のオーナーです」
　ジミーはホテルへ行き、ラルフ・D・スペンサーと名乗って、部屋をとった。ホテルの男に、仕事を始めるためにエルモアに来たのだと告げ、靴の商売はどうだろう、いい靴屋はあるのかと尋ねた。

The man thought that Jimmy's clothes and manners were fine. He was happy to talk to him.

Yes, Elmore needed a good shoe shop. There was no shop that sold just shoes. Shoes were sold in the big shops that sold everything. All business in Elmore was good. He hoped Mr. Spencer would decide to stay in Elmore. It was a pleasant town to live in, and the people were friendly.

Mr. Spencer said he would stay in the town a few days and learn something about it. No, he said, he himself would carry his bag up to his room. He didn't want a boy to take it. It was very heavy.

Mr. Ralph Spencer remained in Elmore. He started a shoe shop. Business was good.

Also, he made many friends. And he was successful with the wish of his heart. He met Annabel Adams. He liked her better every day.

■be happy to ～ 喜んで～する　■sell just　～だけを専門に販売する　■want A to ～
Aに～して欲しい　■wish of one's heart 心からの望み

ホテルの男には、ジミーが身につけているものやマナーが洗練されているように思えた。そこで、彼は喜んでジミーに話した。

　「ええ。エルモアにはいい靴屋が必要なんです。靴だけを売っている店はないんです。靴は、何でもかんでも売っている大きな店で売られていますよ。ここでは、どんな商売もうまくいきますよ。スペンサーさんにエルモアにずっといていただければよろしいのですが。住むには快適な町ですよ。人間も親切ですしね」

　スペンサー氏は、2、3日滞在して、町についていろいろ勉強してみようと答えた。いや、バッグは自分で部屋に運ぶ、ボーイに運んでほしくはない、とても重いから、とも言った。

　ラルフ・スペンサー氏はエルモアに留まり、靴屋を始めた。商売は順調だった。

　そのうえ、沢山の友だちができた。そして、心のうちで望んでいたこともうまくいった。アナベル・アダムズに会ったのだ。日を追うごとに、彼女のことが好きになっていった。

At the end of a year everyone in Elmore liked Mr. Ralph Spencer. His shoe shop was doing very good business. And he and Annabel were going to be married in two weeks. Mr. Adams, the small-town banker, liked Spencer. Annabel was very proud of him. He seemed already to belong to the Adams family.

One day Jimmy sat down in his room to write this letter, which he sent to one of his old friends:

Dear Old Friend:

I want you to meet me at Sullivan's place next week, on the evening of the 10th. I want to give you my tools. I know you'll be glad to have them. You couldn't buy them for a thousand dollars. I finished with the old business—— a year ago. I have a nice shop. I'm living a better life, and I'm going to marry the best girl on earth two weeks from now. It's the only life——I wouldn't ever again touch another man's money. After I marry, I'm going to go further west, where I'll never see anyone who knew me in my old life. I tell you, she's a wonderful girl. She trusts me.

Your old friend,
Jimmy.

■belong to ～に属する　■Dear ～ 親愛なる～へ、拝啓～様　■the best ～ on earth 世界最高の～　■It's the only life. たった一つの（かけがえのない）人生だ。

その年が終わるころには、ラルフ・スペンサー氏はエルモアの誰からも好かれていた。靴店は大いに繁盛していた。そして、ジミーとアナベルは2週間後に結婚することになった。小さな町の銀行家のアダムズ氏は、ジミーを気に入っていた。アナベルは彼のことを誇りに思っていた。彼は、すでにアダムズ家の一員のようなものだった。

　ある日、ジミーは自分の部屋で次のような手紙をしたため、旧友のひとりに送った。

　懐かしい友へ、

　来週、10日の夕方、サリヴァンのところであんたに会いたい。おれの道具一式をあんたに譲りたい。あんたは喜んでそれをもらってくれるだろうと思っている。この道具一式は、1000ドル出しても手に入らないだろうよ。おれは、1年前に足を洗ったんだ。今は、立派な店を持っている。前よりましな生活を送っている。2週間後には、世界で一番かわいい娘と結婚するんだ。最高の人生だ。おれは二度と他人の金に手を出すようなことはしないつもりだ。結婚したら、昔のおれを知っている人間に会うことがないところ、つまり、もっと西へ行くつもりだ。本当に、彼女は素敵なんだ。おれを信じてくれている。

古くからの友、

ジミーより

On the Monday night after Jimmy sent this letter, Ben Price arrived quietly in Elmore. He moved slowly about the town in his quiet way, and learned all that he wanted to know. Standing inside a shop, he watched Ralph D. Spencer walk by.

"You're going to marry the banker's daughter, are you, Jimmy?" said Ben to himself. "I don't feel sure about that!"

09

The next morning Jimmy was at the Adams home. He was going to a nearby city that day to buy new clothes for the wedding. He was also going to buy a gift for Annabel. It would be his first trip out of Elmore. It was more than a year now since he had done any safe-breaking.

Most of the Adams family went to the bank together that morning. There were Mr. Adams, Annabel, Jimmy, and Annabel's married sister with her two little girls, aged five and nine. They passed Jimmy's hotel, and Jimmy ran up to his room and brought along his bag. Then they went to the bank.

All went inside——Jimmy, too, for he was one of the family. Everyone in the bank was glad to see the good-looking, nice young man who was going to marry Annabel. Jimmy put down his bag.

■walk by 通りかかる ■feel sure 確信する ■run up to ～まで駆け上がる ■bring along 携えていく ■be glad to ～して嬉しい

ジミーがこの手紙を投函した月曜日の夜、ベン・プライスは密かにエルモアに到着した。彼なりの静かなやりかたで、町をゆっくりぶらつき、知りたいことについて、あらゆる情報を得た。一軒の店の中から、ラルフ・D・スペンサーが通り過ぎるのを注意深く見守っていた。

　「おまえさん、銀行家の娘と結婚するんだってな、ジミー？　さて、それはどうかな」とひとりごちた。

　翌朝、ジミーはアダムズ家にいた。その日彼は、結婚式のために新しい洋服を買いに近くの街に出かける予定であった。彼はまた、アナベルへのプレゼントも買うつもりだった。エルモアに来て以来、初めての旅行であった。最後の金庫破りから1年以上たっていた。

　その朝、アダムズ家の人たちがそろって銀行へ出かけた。アダムズ氏、アナベル、ジミー、アナベルの結婚している姉と彼女の5歳と9歳の娘たちであった。ジミーは、滞在しているホテルを通り過ぎるとき、自分の部屋へ駆け上がり、バッグをとってきた。それから、みなで銀行に向かった。

　ジミーも含めて全員が銀行に入った。いまや彼は家族の一員なのだ。銀行では誰もが、アナベルと結婚することになっているハンサムで感じのいい青年に会えて喜んだ。ジミーはバッグを下においた。

Annabel, laughing, put Jimmy's hat on her head and picked up the bag. "How do I look?" she asked. "Ralph, how heavy this bag is! It feels full of gold."

"It's full of some things I don't need in my shop," Jimmy said. "I'm taking them to the city, to the place where they came from. That saves me the cost of sending them. I'm going to be a married man. I must learn to save money."

The Elmore bank had a new safe. Mr. Adams was very proud of it, and he wanted everyone to see it. It was as large as a small room, and it had a very special door. The door was controlled by a clock. Using the clock, the banker planned the time when the door should open. At other times no one, not even the banker himself, could open it. He explained about it to Mr. Spencer. Mr. Spencer seemed interested but he did not seem to understand very easily. The two children, May and Agatha, enjoyed seeing the shining heavy door, with all its special parts.

■How ～ A is! Aはなんて～なんだろう！　■It feels ～ . ～な感じがします。　■take A to ～　Aを～に持っていく　■seem to　～のように見える

アナベルは、笑いながら、ジミーの帽子をかぶり、バッグを持ち上げた。「わたし、どう見える？」とアナベルが言った。「ラルフ、このバッグ、なんて重いんでしょう。金がいっぱい詰まっているみたい」

　「ぼくの店では必要のないものが詰まっているんだよ。それを大きな町に持っていくつもりなんだ。それがもともとあったところさ。そうすると、送る費用が節約できるだろ。ぼくはまもなくしたら夫になるんだ。金を節約することも学ぶ必要があるよね」

　エルモア銀行には新式の金庫があった。アダムズ氏はその金庫を大いに自慢し、誰かれとなく見せたがった。大きさは小さな部屋ほどで、非常に特殊な扉がついていた。扉は時計で制御され、オーナーのアダムズ氏が時計を使って、扉が開く時間を設定する仕組みであった。ほかの時間には、たとえオーナーであれ、扉を開けることはできなかった。アダムズ氏はこういったことをスペンサー氏に説明した。スペンサー氏は、興味をもったようであったが、即座に理解したようには見えなかった。子どもたちのメイとアガサは、特殊な部品が付いた、きらきらと光っている重い扉をみて面白がった。

While they were busy like this, Ben Price entered the bank and looked around. He told a young man who worked there that he had not come on business; he was waiting for a man.

Suddenly there was a cry from the women. They had not been watching the children. May, the nine-year-old girl, had playfully but firmly closed the door of the safe. And Agatha was inside.

The old banker tried to open the door. He pulled at it for a moment. "The door can't be opened," he cried. "And the clock——I hadn't started it yet."

Agatha's mother cried out again.

"Quiet!" said Mr. Adams, raising a shaking hand. "All be quiet for a moment. Agatha!" he called as loudly as he could. "Listen to me." They could hear, but not clearly, the sound of the child's voice. In the darkness inside the safe, she was wild with fear.

"My baby!" her mother cried. "She will die of fear! Open the door! Break it open! Can't you men do something?"

■on business 商用で、仕事で ■wild 形 ひどく興奮した ■die of fear 恐怖のあまり死ぬ

みながこういったことに気をとられている最中に、ベン・プライスが
銀行に入ってきてあたりを見回した。彼は若い銀行員に、仕事で来たの
ではなくある男を待っているんだ、と告げた。

　突如、女性たちから悲鳴があがった。彼女たちは子どもたちから目を
離していた。9歳になるメイが、面白半分に、しかししっかりと金庫の
扉を閉めてしまったのだ。そしてアガサは金庫の中にいる。

　老アダムズ氏は扉を開けようとして、少しの間、扉をつかんで引っ
張った。「扉は開けられない」アダムズ氏は叫んだ。「時計は——わしは、
まだ時間を設定してないんだよ」

　アガサの母親が悲鳴を上げた。

　「静かに！」アダムズ氏は手を振りながら叫んだ。「みなさん、少しの
あいだ静かにしてもらいたい。アガサ！」アダムズ氏はできるかぎりの
声を張り上げて、呼びかけた。「おじいちゃんの言うとおりにするんだ
よ」子どもの声が聞こえたが、はっきりとではなかった。金庫の暗闇の
なかで、アガサは恐怖で見境なく泣き叫んでいた。

　「ああ、アガサ！」母親が叫んだ。「アガサは恐ろしさのあまり死んで
しまうわ！ 扉を開けて！ 扉を壊して！ みなさん、どうにかできない
の？」

"There isn't a man nearer than the city who can open that door," said Mr. Adams, in a shaking voice. "My God! Spencer, what shall we do? That child——she can't live long in there. There isn't enough air. And the fear will kill her."

Agatha's mother, wild too now, beat on the door with her hands. Annabel turned to Jimmy, her large eyes full of pain, but with some hope, too. A woman thinks that the man she loves can somehow do any thing.

"Can't you do something, Ralph? Try, won't you?"

He looked at her with a strange soft smile on his lips and in his eyes.

"Annabel," he said, "give me that flower you are wearing, will you?"

She could not believe that she had really heard him. But she put the flower in his hand. Jimmy took it and put it where he could not lose it. Then he pulled off his coat. With that act, Ralph D. Spencer passed away and Jimmy Valentine took his place.

"Stand away from the door, all of you," he commanded.

■My God! 神よ！なんてことだ！ ■somehow 副 どうにかして ■pull off 脱ぐ
■pass away 消え去る ■take one's place（人と）交代する ■Stand away from ～.
～から離れてください。

「この扉を開けることができる人間は、この町の近くにはいないんだ」。アダムズ氏はふるえる声で言った。「おお、神様！ スペンサー、どうしたらよいのだろう？ あの子は、アガサは金庫の中で長くは生きていられまい。十分な空気がないのだ。そして恐怖で死んでしまうだろう」

アガサの母親も、狂ったように手で扉を叩いた。アナベルは、ジミーのほうへ振りかえった。大きな目は苦悩に満ちていたが、なにか希望ものぞかせていた。女性というものは、愛する男が、とにかく何かをしてくれると考えるものである。

「どうにかならないかしら、ラルフ？ ためしてみて」

ジミーは、唇と目に奇妙な穏やかな笑みを浮かべて、アナベルを見た。

「アナベル、きみが身につけているその花をぼくにくれないか?」ジミーは言った。

アナベルは、ジミーが言ったことが信じられなかったが、彼の手に花を渡した。ジミーは花を受け取って、なくさない場所にしまった。それからコートを脱いだ。この行為で、ラルフ・D・スペンサーは姿を消し、替わってジミー・ヴァレンタインが姿を現したのだ。

「みなさん、扉から離れてください」ジミーは命じた。

He put his bag on the table and opened it flat. From that time on, he seemed not to know that anyone else was near. Quickly he laid the shining strange tools on the table. The others watched as if they had lost the power to move.

In a minute Jimmy was at work on the door. In ten minutes——faster than he had ever done it before——he had the door open.

Agatha was taken into her mother's arms.

Jimmy Valentine put on his coat, picked up the flower and walked toward the front door. As he went he thought he heard a voice call, "Ralph!" He did not stop.

At the door a big man stood in his way.

"Hello, Ben!" said Jimmy, still with his strange smile. "You're here at last, are you? Let's go. I don't care, now."

And then Ben Price acted rather strangely.

"I guess you're wrong about this, Mr. Spencer," he said. "I don't believe I know you, do I?"

And Ben Price turned and walked slowly down the street.

■from that time on それ以後 ■In a minute すぐに ■at work 仕事中で ■take into one's arms 抱きしめる ■stand in one's way 行く手に立ちふさがる ■be wrong about ~のことを誤解する

彼は、バッグをテーブルに置き、開けた。それからというもの、誰か他の人間が近くにいることにも気づいていない様子だった。素早く、テーブルの上に、きらきら光る不思議な道具を並べた。他のものたちは、身じろぎもせずにその道具を見つめた。

　すぐにジミーは、扉の作業にとりかかった。10分後――これまでのどの場合よりも短かった――ジミーは扉を開けた。

　アガサは母親の腕に抱かれた。

　ジミー・ヴァレンタインはコートを着て、花を拾いあげ、正面のドアへ向かった。途中、「ラルフ！」という呼び声を聞いたと思ったが、立ち止まることはなかった。

　正面ドアのところに、大男が行く手をはばむように立っていた。

　「やあ、ベン！」依然として、奇妙な笑みを浮かべてジミーは言った。「やっと、ここに来たな。行こう。もう、どうでもいいんだ」

　すると、ベン・プライスは、信じられないような行動にでた。

　「なにか誤解しているようですよ、スペンサーさん。わたしは、あなたを知っているとは思いませんが」

　そして、ベン・プライスは踵を返して、通りをゆっくりと歩いて行った。

覚えておきたい英語表現

　retrieve は「取り戻す、救出する、償う」という意味ですが、表題には「（猟犬が）逃げようとする獲物を取ってくる」find and bring back という意味合いも込められているようです。reformation は「改心、矯正」という意味ですね。

　出所後に心を入れ替えて正業につこうとした金庫破りの名人が刑事に尾行される状況の中で、人命救助のために凄腕を働かせてしまう……ところがドンデン返しのような結末が待ちかまえていたという物語です。

The five dollars were supposed to help him become a better man.
（p.94, 2-3行目）

この5ドルは、彼がもっとましな人間になるのに役立てられるはずであった。

【解説】supposeは「想定する、暗に意味する」という意味の動詞。be supposed to do...は、「…することになっている」という意味です。You are supposed to be here at eight.（君は8時出勤ということになっている）

> Mike enjoyed these words so much that Jimmy had to take a drink with him. (p.98, 8-9行目)
>
> マイクはジミーのことばをひどく面白がり、ジミーは彼と一杯飲むはめになった。

【解説】ここはいわゆるso ～ that構文ですね。「あまりに～なので…」と訳します。つまり直訳すると、「マイクがジミーのことばをあまりに面白がったので、ジミーは彼と一杯飲むはめになった」という意味です。

> In a minute Jimmy was at work on the door. In ten minutes—faster than he had ever done it before—he had the door open.
> (p.116, 5-7行目)
>
> すぐにジミーは、扉の作業にとりかかった。10分後――これまでのどの場合よりも短かった――ジミーは扉を開けた。

【解説】時間的経過を表すinを重ねて使うことによって、この場面の緊迫感がうまく演出されていますね。

前置詞inには多様な意味がありますが、ここで使われているような「時間的経過を表す」用法は頻出表現ですので、必ずマスターしておきましょう。

【時間的経過を表すinの用法】

1、～（のうち）に、～の間、～中

in a minute, in a moment　すぐに

2、〈未来を表す〉～たてば、～の後には

She'll be in a office in a few minutes.
彼女は2～3分後には出社するでしょう。

3、～の間で

the coldest day in five years　この5年間でいちばんの寒さ

After Twenty Years

20年後

The cop moved along the street, looking strong and important. This was the way he always moved. He was not thinking of how he looked. There were few people on the street to see him. It was only about ten at night, but it was cold. And there was a wind with a little rain in it.

He stopped at doors as he walked along, trying each door to be sure that it was closed for the night. Now and then he turned and looked up and down the street. He was a fine-looking cop, watchful, guarding the peace.

People in this part of the city went home early. Now and then you might see the lights of a shop or of a small restaurant. But most of the doors belonged to business places that had been closed hours ago.

■walk along 歩く ■be sure that 〜 必ず〜のようにする ■now and then ときどき ■look up and down あちこちを見る ■business place 事務所

その警官は、断固とした重々しい様子で、通りを歩いていた。彼は、いつもこんな風にして歩いていた。自分がどんな風に見えているのか、頭になかった。その通りで、彼を見かける人間は、ほとんどいなかった。まだ夜の10時ごろだったが、寒く、そのうえ、風が吹き、小雨が降っていた。

　彼は歩いているときも、ドアのところで立ち止まっては、それぞれのドアが夜のあいだしっかり閉まっているかどうか確認しようとしていた。ときどき振り返り、通りを見回した。彼は、体格のいい警官で、油断なく、平和を守っているのだ。

　ニューヨークのこの地域の人たちは、家へ帰るのが早い。時折、店や小さなレストランの灯りが目につくが、ほとんどが事務所のドアなので、何時間も前に閉められてしまう。

Then the cop suddenly slowed his walk. Near the door of a darkened shop a man was standing. As the cop walked toward him, the man spoke quickly.

"It's all right, officer," he said. "I'm waiting for a friend. Twenty years ago we agreed to meet here tonight. It sounds strange to you, doesn't it? I'll explain if you want to be sure that everything's all right. About twenty years ago there was a restaurant where this shop stands. "Big Joe Brady's Restaurant."

"It was here until five years ago," said the cop. The man near the door had a colorless square face with bright eyes, and a little white mark near his right eye. He had a large jewel in his necktie.

"Twenty years ago tonight," said the man, "I had dinner here with Jimmy Wells. He was my best friend and the best fellow in the world. He and I grew up together here in New York, like two brothers. I was eighteen and Jimmy was twenty. The next morning I was to start for the West. I was going to find a job and make a great success. You couldn't have pulled Jimmy out of New York. He thought it was the only place on earth.

■officer 图 警官　■agree to ～することに同意する　■sound strange 異様に聞こえる　■mark 图（傷などの）跡　■pull A out of ～ Aを～から離す

そのとき、突然、警官の歩みが遅くなった。灯りが落ちた店のドアの近くに、男が一人立っていた。その警官が男に近づくと、すぐに男は話しかけてきた。

　「なんでもありませんぜ、おまわりさん。友だちを待っているんで。20年前、今夜ここで会うことにしたんだ。おかしいかい？　まったく真っ当だと、確かめたいなら、説明するよ。20年ほど前、この店があるところにレストランがあったんだ。ビッグ・ジョー・ブレディ・レストランといった」

　「5年前までここにあったよ」と警官が答えた。ドア近くの男は、血の気のない角ばった顔に、目を光らせ、右目近くに小さな白っぽい傷痕があった。ネクタイには大きな宝石がついていた。

　「20年前の今夜、おれはジミー・ウェルズと一緒にここで晩飯を食ったんだ。ジミーは、おれの親友で、世界で最高のヤツさ。おれたちは、ここニューヨークで兄弟のようにして大きくなった。おれは18歳、ジミーは20歳だった。翌朝、おれは西部に向けて発つことになっていた。仕事を見つけて、大成功するつもりだったんだ。誰もジミーをニューヨークから引っ張り出すことはできなかった。ヤツは、ここが地球で一番の場所と思っていたんだな。

"We agreed that night that we would meet here again in twenty years. We thought that in twenty years we would know what kind of men we were, and what future waited for us."

"It sounds interesting," said the cop. "A long time between meetings, it seems to me. Have you heard from your friend since you went West?"

"Yes, for a time we did write to each other," said the man. "But after a year or two, we stopped. The West is big. I moved around everywhere, and I moved quickly. But I know that Jimmy will meet me here if he can. He was as true as any man in the world. He'll never forget. I came a thousand miles to stand here tonight. But I'll be glad about that, if my old friend comes too."

The waiting man took out a fine watch, covered with small jewels.

"Three minutes before ten," he said. "It was ten that night when we said good-bye here at the restaurant door."

"You were successful in the West, weren't you?" asked the cop.

■hear from ～から連絡をもらう　■write to each other 文通をする　■a year or two
1～2年　■as ～ as any A どんなAよりも～な

その晩、おれたちは20年後、ここで会おうと約束したんだ。おれたちがどんな男なっているのか、どんな未来が待ちうけていたのか、20年後にはわかるだろうと思ってね」

「面白いな」と警官が言った。「おれには、その再会までの期間は長そうに思えるな。あんたが西部に行ったあと、あんたの友だちから便りはあったのかな」

「もちろんさ。しばらくは手紙のやり取りをしていた。だが、1、2年もするとやめてしまった。西部は広い。おれはあちこち動き回った。それも素早くだ。それでも、おれにはわかるんだ。ジミーはここでおれに会うんだとな。ヤツは世界で一番信頼できる男だった。あいつは決して忘れない。おれは今夜ここに立つために、千マイルも離れたところから来たのさ。それで、友だちが来てくれたら、嬉しいよ」

　待つ男は、小さな宝石で覆われた、素晴らしい時計を取り出した。

「10時3分前だ」男は言った。「あの夜、おれたちが、レストランのドアがあったここで別れたのは10時だった」

「あんたは西部で成功したんだな」警官は尋ねた。

"I surely was! I hope Jimmy has done half as well. He was a slow mover. I've had to fight for my success. In New York a man doesn't change much. In the West you learn how to fight for what you get."

The cop took a step or two.

"I'll go on my way," he said. "I hope your friend comes all right. If he isn't here at ten, are you going to leave?"

"I am not!" said the other. "I'll wait half an hour, at least. If Jimmy is alive on earth, he'll be here by that time. Good night, officer."

"Good night," said the cop, and walked away, trying doors as he went.

There was now a cold rain falling and the wind was stronger. The few people walking along that street were hurrying, trying to keep warm. And at the door of the shop stood the man who had come a thousand miles to meet a friend. Such a meeting could not be certain. But he waited.

About twenty minutes he waited, and then a tall man in a long coat came hurrying across the street. He went directly to the waiting man.

■slow mover のろま　■take a step or two　一歩か二歩踏み出す　■go on one's way 出発する　■on earth　この世で　■try door　ドアを（鍵がかかっているか）確認する

「そうさ！ ジミーがおれの半分ほども成功していてくれたらと思うよ。ヤツは愚図だったからね。成功するためには、闘う必要があったよ。ニューヨークでは、人ってそんなに変わることはないね。西部では、なにかを手に入れるための闘い方をおぼえるんだ」

警官は1、2歩、後へ下がった。

「行かなくては。あんたの友だちが無事に来ることを祈っているよ。もし友だちが10時に来なければ、行ってしまうのかい？」

「とんでもない！ 少なくても30分は待つつもりだ。ジミーがこの世に生きているなら、そのころまでには来るだろうよ。じゃあな、おまわりさん」

「おやすみ」と警官は言って、行きがてらドアを1つ1つ確認しながら、去って行った。

冷たい雨は降り続き、風が強まってきていた。数少ない通行人たちは先を急ぎ、寒さから逃れようとしていた。店の入り口には、千マイルも離れたところから来た男が、友だちに会うために立っていた。会えるかどうか定かではなかったが、男は待った。

20分ほど待った。すると、長いコートを着た背の高い男が、通りを横切って急ぎ足でやって来た。その男は、まっすぐ、待っている男の方に来た。

"Is that you, Bob?" he asked, doubtfully.

"Is that you, Jimmy Wells?" cried the man at the door.

The new man took the other man's hands in his. "It's Bob! It's surely is. I was certain I would find you here if you were still alive. Twenty years is a long time. The old restaurant is gone, Bob. I wish it were here, so that we could have another dinner in it. Has the West been good to you?"

"It gave me everything I asked for. You've changed, Jimmy. I never thought you were so tall."

"Oh, I grew a little after I was twenty."

"Are you doing well in New York, Jimmy?"

"Well enough. I work for the city. Come on, Bob. We'll go to a place I know, and have a good long talk about old times."

The two men started along the street, arm in arm. The man from the West was beginning to tell the story of his life. The other, with his coat up to his ears, listened with interest.

At the corner stood a shop bright with electric lights. When they came near, each turned to look at the other's face.

The man from the West stopped suddenly and pulled his arm away.

■I wish + 主語 + 過去形　〜だったら良かったのになあ。　■so that 〜できるように
■arm in arm 腕を組んで　■pull 〜 away 〜を引き離す

「おまえ、ボブなのか?」疑わしそうに尋ねた。

「おまえ、ジミー・ウェルズか?」ドアのところの男は叫んだ。

新しく来た男は、相手の男の手をとった。「確かにボブだ! おまえが生きているなら、必ずここで会えると思っていたよ。20年は長かったな。昔のレストランはなくなってしまったよ、ボブ。あのレストランがここにあったらいいのになあ。そしたら、一緒に夕飯を食うことができたのに。西部ではうまくいったのか?」

「おれが欲しかったものはすべて手に入れた。おまえは変わったな、ジミー。そんなに背が高かったとは思わなかったよ」

「ああ、20歳を過ぎて少し伸びたんだ」

「ニューヨークではうまくやっているのか、ジミー」

「うまくやっているよ。市の仕事をしているんだ。さあ、ボブ。おれの知っているところで、昔のことをいろいろ話そうぜ」

2人の男は、腕を組んで、通りを歩き始めた。西部から来た男は、これまでの自分の人生について語り始めた。もう1人の男は、耳までコートを引き上げて、興味深げに話を聞いていた。

街角に電灯で明るく照らされた店があった。その近くに来たとき、2人は向きを変えて、相手の顔を見た。

西部からの男は急に立ち止まり、手を振りほどいた。

"You're not Jimmy Wells," he said. "Twenty years is a long time, but not long enough to change the shape of a man's nose."

"It sometimes changes a good man into a bad one," said the tall man. "You've been under arrest for ten minutes, Bob. Chicago cops thought you might be coming to New York. They told us to watch for you. Are you coming with me quietly? That's wise. But first here is something I was asked to give you. You may read it here at the window. It's from a cop named Wells."

The man from the West opened the little piece of paper. His hand began to shake a little as he read.

"Bob: I was at the place on time. I saw the face of the man wanted by Chicago cops. I didn't want to arrest you myself. So I went and got another cop and sent him to do the job.

JIMMY."

■change A into B　AをBに変える　■under arrest　逮捕されて　■on time　時間通りに　■wanted by　指名手配を受けている

「おまえ、ジミー・ウェルズではないな」男は言った。「20年は長かったが、鼻の形が変わるほど長くはないぞ」

「20年という年月は、いいヤツを悪人にすることもあるのさ」背の高い男は言った。「10分前から、おまえは逮捕されているんだ、ボブ。シカゴ警察は、おまえがニューヨークに現れると考えていた。ヤツらは、おれたちにおまえを見張るように言ってきたのさ。おとなしく、おれと来るか？ それが賢明だ。だが、その前におまえに渡すように頼まれたものがある。窓のところで読むといい。ウェルズという警官からだ」

西部からの男は、小さな紙片を開いた。読み進むにつれ、手が少し震え始めた。

「ボブへ：おれは時間どおりにあの場所にいた。そしてシカゴ警察が指名手配している男の顔を見たのだ。おれは、自分の手でおまえを逮捕したくなかった。そこで、他の警官を探しに行ってお前を逮捕してもらった。

　　　　　　　　　　　　　　　　　　　　ジミー」

覚えておきたい英語表現

　　説明するまでもなく日本人にはよく知られているオー・ヘンリーの名
作ですね。20年という時が2人の旧友の人生をくっきりと分け、2度と
交わりようもないものにしてしまった。「再会」した一瞬の光景が目に
浮かぶようです。10年間なら decade、約30年（一世代）なら generation
という単語が別にありますが、20年というのは不安定なある意味では
残酷な時の流れなのかも知れません。熟年離婚も結婚20年後がピーク
のようですし……。

The cop moved along the street, looking strong and important.
（p.122, 1-2行目）
その警官は、断固とした重々しい様子で、通りを歩いていた。

【解説】みなさんもよくご存知の通り、look は前置詞 at を伴って「〜を見る、眺める」
という意味でよく使われますが、ここでは look の後に形容詞が補語としてくっつい
ています。この場合、「〈顔つき、様子が〉〜に見える、思われる」という意味になる
ことに注意しましょう。同時に、look like ＋名詞、動名詞「〜のように見える、思
われる」の語法も覚えてください。

　　　　You look pale. 　顔色がよくないですね。

　　　　It looks like rain. 　雨になりそうです。

It sounds strange to you, doesn't it? （p.124, 5-6行目）
おかしいかい？

"It sounds interesting," said the cop. （p.126, 4行目）
「面白いな」と警官が言った。

【解説】どちらのsoundも「音がする（出る）」と言う意味ではなく、補語を伴って「～のように見える、思われる」つまりseem, appearという意味になります。

The next morning I was to start for the West. （p.124, 下から4行目）
翌朝、おれは西部に向けて発つことになっていた。

【解説】be動詞＋to不定詞の構文には、一般的に５つの意味があります。予定・義務・可能・運命・意図ですが、ここは予定の意味です。The next morning I was going to start for the West.と言い換えることができます。

Yes, for a time we did write to each other. （p.126, 7行目）
もちろんさ。しばらくは（本当に）手紙のやり取りをしていた。

【解説】このdid（do）は、動詞の意味を強調している助動詞です。

I do think so. 僕も本当にそう思う

Transients in Arcadia

アルカディアの休日

There is a certain hotel on Broadway that is very pleasant in the summer. Not many people have heard about it. It is wide and cool. Its rooms have walls of dark wood. There are green trees around it, and soft winds. It has all the pleasures of mountain living and none of the pains. You will eat better fish than you could catch for yourself in streams in the hills. You will have better meat than a hunter brings home from the forest.

A few have discovered this cool spot in the hot summer of New York. You will see these few guests eating dinner in the hotel restaurant. They are happy to be there and happy to know that they are very few. They feel especially wise because they have found this delightful place.

■certain 形 とある　■hear about ～について知る　■none of ～ 少しの～もない
■stream 名 小川　■delightful 形 快適な

ブロードウェイに、夏に非常に快適なホテルがあった。そのホテル
は、多くの人に知られているわけではなかった。広々として、ひんやり
としていた。それぞれの部屋の壁は黒っぽい木でできていた。ホテルの
周囲には、緑の木々が茂り、心地よい風が吹き抜けた。ホテルには、山
で暮らすようなありとあらゆる快適さがあり、およそ不快さとは無縁で
あった。そこでは、丘を流れる小川で自ら獲る魚よりもうまい魚が食べ
られるし、狩人が森で獲って来る肉よりもうまい肉を食べることができ
た。

　少数の人だけが、ニューヨークの暑い夏に、この涼しげな場所を見
つけていたのだ。ホテルのレストランでは、ディナーを食べているこ
ういった客を目にすることだろう。彼らは、ここにいることに幸せを感
じ、数少ない客の一人であることに満足感をおぼえていた。彼らは、こ
の快適な場所を見つけて、自分は賢明だと思っているのだ。

More waiters than necessary are always near. They bring what is wanted before anyone asks for it.

The pleasing distant noise of Broadway sounds like running water in a forest. At every strange footstep, the guests turn quickly and look. They are afraid that the restless pleasure-seekers will find their hotel and destroy its pleasant quiet.

And so these few live during the hot season. They enjoy the delights of mountain and sea shore. All is brought to them in their Broadway hotel.

This summer a lady came to the hotel giving this name: "Madame Héloise D'Arcy Beaumont."

The name was like a name in the story of a great romance. And Madame Beaumont was the kind of lady the Hotel Lotus loved. She was beautiful and her manner was very fine. Everyone wished to serve her. The other guests believed that as a guest she was perfection.

This perfect guest did not often leave the hotel. In this, she was like the other guests of the Hotel Lotus. To enjoy that hotel, one needed to forget the city. New York might have been miles away. At night sometimes one might go out. But during the hot day one remained in the cool shade of the Lotus.

■sound like 〜のように聞こえる　■strange 形 知らない、馴染みのない　■give one's name 名を名乗る　■serve 動 給仕をする　■one 代 人、だれでも

必要以上の数のウェイターが、いつでも近くに控えている。彼らは、客が頼むまえに、それと察して、客が要求するものを持ってきてくれる。

　ブロードウェイから流れてくるかすかな心地よいざわめきは、森を流れる水のように響いていた。聞きなれない足音がするたびに、客たちはサッと振り返って見るのだった。ホテルが、せわしなく動き回る行楽客に見つかり、心地よい静けさが台無しにされるのではないかと、心配しているのだ。

　そこで、これらの少数の人たちは、暑い夏のあいだここに滞在し、山や海辺の心地よさを享受する。このブロードウェイのホテルでは、そのすべてが与えられるのだ。

　この夏、名前をエロイーズ・ダーシー・ボーモン夫人というレディがやって来た。

　大ロマンス小説の登場人物のような名前であった。そして、ボーモン夫人は、ホテル・ロータス好みのレディであった。夫人は美しく、マナーはたいそう洗練されていた。誰もが、夫人の給仕をしたがった。他の客たちは、夫人がホテルの客として完璧であると認めた。

　この完璧な客が、ホテルから出かけることは滅多になかった。こういった点でも、夫人はホテルの他の滞在客と変わらなかった。ホテルを楽しむためには、ニューヨークという市を忘れる必要があった。ニューヨークは数マイルも遠くにあるのだと思えばいいのだ。ときには夜出かける人も、暑い日中には、ロータスの涼しげな日陰に留まっていた。

Madame was alone in the Hotel Lotus. She was alone as a queen is alone, because of her high position. She rose from bed late in the morning. She was then a sweet, soft person who seemed to shine quietly.

But at dinner she was different. She would wear a beautiful dress. I cannot find words fine enough to tell about it. Always there were red flowers at her shoulder. When the head waiter saw a dress like this, he met it at the door. You thought of Paris when you saw it, and of the theater and of old romances.

A story about Madame Beaumont was told among the guests in the Hotel Lotus. It was said that she was a woman who had traveled all over the world. It was said that she knew the most important people everywhere. It was said that in her white hands she held the future of certain nations.

It was no surprise, they said, that such a lady should choose the Hotel Lotus. It was the most desirable and the most restful place in America during the heat of summer.

■would 助（よく）〜したものだった《（過去の）習慣》 ■fine enough to 〜するのに充分な ■It is said that 〜. 〜であると言われている。 ■hold the future 将来を左右する ■It is no surprise that 〜. 〜は驚くにあたらない。

夫人はロータス・ホテルでは一人ぼっちだった。女王がその高い地位のために孤独であるように、夫人も孤独であった。朝は遅くまでベッドから出ることはなかった。夫人は、美しく、もの静かで、その様子は静かに光を放っているようであった。

　だが、夕食のときには違っていた。いつも美しいドレスを身につけていた。それは形容しがたいほど美しいドレスであった。肩には、いつも赤い花をつけていた。給仕頭はこういったドレスを目にすると、ドアのところで出迎えた。そのドレスは、パリや劇場、古い恋物語を思い起こさせるのだった。

　ボーモン夫人についての物語がホテル・ロータスの泊り客のあいだで語られた。夫人は世界中を旅している女性で、各地の最重要人物と懇意であると言われた。ある国々の命運は夫人の白い手に握られているとも噂された。

　客たちによると、このような女性が、ホテル・ロータスを選ぶのは意外ではないのだそうだ。暑熱の夏のあいだ、アメリカでもっとも理想的で休息のできる場所は、ホテル・ロータスをおいて他にないということだ。

On the third day of Madame Beaumont's stay in the hotel, a young man entered as a guest. His clothes were quiet but good. His face was pleasant. His expression was that of a man who had traveled and could understand the world. He said that he would remain three or four days. He asked about the sailing of certain ships. He seemed to like this hotel the best of all he had known.

The young man put his name on the list of hotel guests: Harold Farrington. It was a name with a fine sound. And the young man belonged perfectly in the quiet life of the Lotus. In one day he became like all the other guests. Like them he had his table and his waiter. He also had the same fear that the wrong people might suddenly discover this hotel and destroy its peace.

12

After dinner on the next day, Madame Beaumont dropped something as she passed Harold Farrington's table. He picked it up and, following her, returned it. He spoke only a few quiet words as he did this, and she was pleased by his good manners. She knew that he was a gentleman.

■remain 動 滞在する　■put one's name on　〜に名前を書く　■pick 〜 up　〜を拾い上げる　■only a few 〜　ほんの少しの〜

ボーモン夫人がホテルに滞在してから3日目に、若い男がホテルに入ってきた。服装は目立たないが上質であった。感じのいい顔をしていた。顔の表情は、世界を旅し、よく知っている男のそれであった。彼は3、4日滞在したいのだが、と言った。それから、船の出航について尋ねた。彼は、このホテルを、彼が知る限りで最高のホテルとして気に入っているように見えた。

　青年は、ホテルの宿泊客名簿に、ハロルド・ファリントンと名前を記した。響きのいい名前であった。そして、ロータスの静かな生活に完全に溶け込んだ。一日たつと、他の宿泊客と同じようになった。他の人と同じように、青年にもテーブルが定まり、定まったウェイターがついた。彼もまた、場違いな人間が突然このホテル見つけ、平穏さを台無しにするのではと、危惧していた。

　次の日の夕食を済ませて、ボーモン夫人がハロルド・ファリントンのテーブルのそばを通り過ぎたときに、なにかを落とした。ハロルドはそれを拾い上げ、あとを追って、夫人に返した。そのとき、彼は、静かに数語を口にしただけだった。夫人は、彼の洗練されたマナーが気に入った。彼女は、彼が紳士であると納得した。

Guests of the Lotus seemed to understand each other very easily. Perhaps it was the result of having discovered this Broadway hotel. Guests felt sure that only especially fine people would enjoy the cool delights of the Lotus. Now, very quickly, a sudden friendship grew between Farrington and Madame Beaumont. They stood and talked for a few moments.

"I have seen too much of the usual summer hotels," said Madame Beaumont, with a small but sweet smile. "Why go to the mountains or the seashore? We cannot escape noise and dust there. The people who make noise and dust follow us there."

"Even on the ocean," said Farrington sadly, "those same people are all around us. What shall we do when they discover the Lotus?"

"I hope they don't discover the Lotus this week," said Madame. "I know only one other place I like as well. It is the beautiful home of a prince in the mountains in Europe."

"The best people," said Farrington, "are seeking for the quiet places, like this one, where they can escape the crowds."

■result of ～の成果　■for a few moments　しばらくの間　■do too much of ～し過ぎる　■Why do ～？　なぜ（わざわざ）～をするのか（するにはおよばない）　■What shall we do?　どうしましょうか？

ロータスの宿泊客は、いとも容易に互いを理解しあえるようだった。おそらく、それは、同じようにこのブロードウェイのホテルを見つけたことにあるのだろう。宿泊客たちは、ロータスのこの涼しさは格別に素晴らしい人たちだけが享受するものであると、信じていた。いま、それもあっというまに、ファリントンとボーモン夫人のあいだに思いがけない友情が生まれた。2人は立ったまま、数分間、話をしていた。

　「いままで普通の夏のホテルは、それは沢山、拝見してまいりましたの」。かすかな、だが、魅惑的な微笑みを浮かべて、ボーモン夫人が言った。「なぜ、山や海辺に出かけないかですって？　そういったところでは、喧騒や土埃から逃げられませんもの。騒々しくて、土埃を立てている人たちが、わたくしたちの後に付いて回るのですから」

　「海上でさえも」とファリントンが悲しげに言った。「そういった人たちは、われわれの周囲にいるのですよ。ロータスが、そういう人たちに見つけられたらどうしたらいいのでしょうかね」

　「今週はこういう人たちに、ロータスが気づかれないことを願うだけですわ。ここと同じくらい気にいっているところが一つだけありますの。ヨーロッパの山間にある、ある皇族の方の美しいお家ですの」

　「最高の人たちは、このロータスのような静かな場所を探すものです。ここでは、有象無象の人たちから逃げることができますからね」

"I promise myself three more days of this delightful rest," said Madame Beaumont. "The next day my ship sails."

Harold Farrington's eyes showed that he was sorry. "I too must leave then," he said. "But I am not sailing for Europe."

"We cannot stay here forever, though it is so delightful," said Madame Beaumont. "I like it better than my usual life, which is too full of people. I shall never forget my week in the Hotel Lotus."

"Nor shall I," said Farrington in a low voice. "And I shall never like the ship that carries you away."

On their last evening the two sat together at a little table. A waiter brought them something cool to eat.

Madame Beaumont was wearing the same beautiful dress. She seemed thoughtful.

When she had finished eating, she took out a dollar.

■promise myself 心に決める　■though 接 たとえ〜でも　■shall never 〜 決して〜ないだろう　■Nor + 助動詞 + 主語 〜も…ではない《倒置構文》　■carry 〜 away 〜を運び去る

「ここであと3日、素晴らしい休暇を楽しむつもりです。その次の日にわたしの船が出航しますのよ」

ハロルド・ファリントンの目は失望を表していた。「ぼくもその時に、ここを出なければならないんですよ。ですが、ぼくの場合は、ヨーロッパへの向けての船旅ではありませんがね」

「どんなに素晴らしくても、わたくしたちは永遠にここに滞在するわけにはいきませんでしょ。人であふれている、わたくしの日常の生活より、こちらのほうがずっと好きですけど。ホテル・ロータスの1週間を決して忘れませんわ」

「ぼくもですよ」ファリントンは低い声で言った。「それから、あなたを遠くへ連れ去る船を、どうしても好きになれませんね」

最後の晩、2人は一緒に小さなテーブルについた。ウェイターが冷たい食べ物を運んできた。

ボーモン夫人は、例の美しいドレスを身につけ、考えこんでいる様子であった。

食べ終わると、1ドル取り出した。

"Mr. Farrington," she said, with the smile that everyone in the Lotus loved, "I want to tell you something. I'm going to leave early tomorrow morning because I must go back to work. I work selling women's clothes at Casey's shop. That dollar is all the money I have. I won't have more until I get paid at the end of the week. You're a real gentleman, and you've been good to me. I wanted to tell you before I went.

"For a year I've been planning to come here. Each week I put aside a little of my pay, so that I would have enough money. I wanted to live one week like a rich lady. I wanted to get up in the morning when I wished. I wanted to be served by waiters. I wanted to have the best of everything. Now I've done it, and I've been happier than I ever was before. And now I'm going back to work.

"I wanted to tell you about it, Mr. Farrington, because I——I thought you liked me, and I——I liked you. This week I've told you many things that weren't true. I told you things I've read about. They never happened to me. I've been living in a story. It wasn't real. I wanted you to think I was a great lady.

■get paid お金[給料]をもらう ■put aside ～を取っておく ■so that ～できるように ■than I ever was before かつてないほどに ■happen to ～に起こる

「ファリントンさん」夫人は、ロータスの誰もが好きな笑みを浮かべて言った。「お話したいことがありますの。仕事に戻らなければならないので、明日朝早く、ここを出るつもりですの。わたしは、ケイシーの店で、婦人服を売る仕事をしているんです。あのお金はわたしの全財産なんです。週末にお給料をもらうまで、お金は入ってきません。あなたは本当の紳士だし、それにとても親切にしてくださったわ。ここを出る前に、お話しておきたかったんです。

　1年間かけて、ここへ来る計画を立てました。ここへ来るだけのお金ができるよう、毎週、お給料のなかから少しずつ貯めたんです。お金持ちのレディのような暮らしを、1週間だけしてみたかったのよ。朝は好きな時間に起きてみたかったし、ウェイターに給仕されてみたかった。すべて最高のものを経験してみたかった。もう、全部経験したわ。前よりずっと幸せな気分なの。もう、仕事にもどるつもりです。

　ファリントンさん、あなたにこのことをお話ししたかったの。なぜってわたし——あなたが、わたしのことを気にいってくださっていると思ったから、それに——わたしもあなたが好きだから。今週ずっと、本当でないことを沢山あなたに話したわ。みな本で知ったことです。自分で経験したことではないんです。わたしは物語の世界にいて、現実ではなかったの。わたしのことを立派なレディと、思ってほしかったの。

"This dress I'm wearing——it's the only pretty dress I own. I haven't paid for it yet. I'm paying for it a little at a time.

"The price was seventy-five dollars. It was made for me at O'Dowd and Levinsky's shop. I paid ten dollars first, and now I have to pay a dollar a week until it's all paid.

"And that's all I have to say, Mr. Farrington, except that my name is Mamie Siviter, and not Madame Beaumont. Thank you for listening to me. This dollar is the dollar I'm going to pay for my dress tomorrow. And now I'll go up to my room."

As Harold Farrington listened, his face had not changed. When she had finished, he took out a small book and began to write in it. Then he pulled out the small page with his writing on it and gave it to her. And he took the dollar from her hand.

"I go to work too, tomorrow morning," he said. "And I decided to begin now. That paper says you've paid your dollar for this week. I've been working for O'Dowd and Levinsky for three years. Strange, isn't it? We both had the same idea. I always wanted to stay at a good hotel. I get twenty dollars a week. Like you, I put aside a little money at a time until I had enough. Listen, Mamie. Will you go to the pleasure park on Coney Island with me on payday?"

■at a time　一回に　■a dollar a week　週に1ドル　■Will you ～？　～しませんか？
■pleasure park　遊園地　■Coney Island　コニーアイランド《→p.157》　■payday　图
給料日

いま着ているこのドレス、わたしの持っているドレスのなかで唯一きれいな服なんです。まだ支払いは終わっていなくて、1回に少しずつ払っているのよ。

　値段は75ドルでした。オダウド・レヴィンスキーの店で作らせたの。最初10ドル払って、全額払い終えるまで、毎週1ドルずつ払わなければならないんです。

　これでお話ししたいことは全部話したわ、ファリントンさん。それからわたしの名前はマミー・シヴィッター、ボーモン夫人ではありません。聞いてくださってありがとう。この1ドルは、明日、ドレス代として支払うことになっています。もう、自分の部屋に戻ります」

　ハロルド・ファリントンが話を聞いているとき、彼の顔つきは変わらなかった。彼女が話し終えると、ファリントンは小さなノートを取り出し、それに何かを書きつけ始めた。それから書きつけたページを破って彼女に渡し、彼女の手から1ドルを取った。

　「ぼくも明日の朝、仕事に戻ります。そして、今から始めることにしました。その紙には、あなたが今週の1ドルを支払ったと書いてあります。ぼくは、オダウド・レヴィンスキーで3年間働いているんです。不思議ですね。ぼくたちは同じことを考えたなんて。ずっと、ぼくは素晴らしいホテルに泊まりたいと思っていたんです。ぼくの稼ぎは1週間に20ドルで、あなたと同じように、十分な額になるまで少しずつ貯めていたんです。ねえ、マミー。給料日にコニーアイランドの遊園地に行きませんか?」

The girl who had been Madame Héloise D'Arcy Beaumont smiled.

"I'd love to go, Mr. Farrington. Coney will be all right, although we did live here with rich people for a week."

They could hear the night noises of the hot city. Inside the Hotel Lotus it was cool. The waiter stood near, ready to get anything they asked for.

Madame Beaumont started up to her room for the last time.

And he said, "Forget that 'Harold Farrington,' will you? McManus is the name——James McManus. Some call me Jimmy."

"Good night, Jimmy," said Madame.

■I'd love to ~ . ぜひとも～したい。　■ready to いつでも～できる　■up to ～へ行こうとして　■for the last time 最終的に　■some 代 ある[一部] の人々

かつてエロイーズ・ダーシー・ボーモン夫人であった若い女性はにっこり笑った。

　「行きたいわ、ファリントンさん。ここで1週間金持ちの人たちと一緒だったけど、コニーも悪くないわね」

　暑熱の街の夜のざわめきが聞こえていた。ホテル・ロータスの中は涼しかった。ウェイターは、彼らの注文にいつでも応じられるよう、近くに立っていた。

　最後にボーモン夫人は部屋に向かった。

　すると、ファリントンが言った。「ハロルド・ファリントンは忘れてもらえますか。ぼくの名前はマクマナス――ジェームズ・マクマナス。ジミーって呼ぶ人もいます」

　「おやすみなさい、ジミー」夫人は言った。

覚えておきたい英語表現

transientは「短期滞在客」、arcadiaは「桃源郷、理想郷」という意味です。作品の舞台であるHotel Lotusが当時、実在していたかどうかはわかりませんが、調べてみたところニューヨークの五番街とブロードウェイが交差する近くに現在も同じ名前のホテルがありました。しかし、そのホテルは五番街に面していて、何よりも壁が薄いとかシャワーとトイレが共用であるとかの評価で、およそ作品に描かれたような桃源郷には程遠いようでした。

転じてarcadianという単語には「田園趣味の人」という意味があるのですが、ちかごろは「ゲームセンター(game arcade)の常連」という意味もあります。あなたはどちら？

She would wear a beautiful dress.（p.142, 5-6行目）
彼女はいつも美しいドレスを身につけていた。

【解説】このwouldは過去における習慣、習性、反復動作を表し、「よく〜したものだ」の意味になることに注意。なお、この語法はused toで書き換えられるが、多少文語的な趣になります。

After breakfast he would (used to) take a walk in the park.
朝食の後、彼はよく公園を散歩したものだった。

> Why go to the mountains or the seashore? （p.146, 8-9行目）
>
> なぜ、山や海辺に出かけないかですって？

【解説】Why＋原形不定詞の用法に注意しましょう。この語法は、単なる質問ではなく、ある行為に対する理由を問いただしたり、提案・指図・忠告などを示すときに使われます。また、この語法は、Why don't you go to the mountains or the seashore?　というふうに、notを伴う修辞疑問の形で書き換えができます。

> I promise myself three more days of this delightful rest. （p.148, 1行目）
>
> ここであと3日、素晴らしい休暇を楽しむつもりです。

【解説】promise oneselfは、「…を心待ちにする、楽しみに待つ、…するつもりでいる」という意味です。She promised herself that she'd never see him again.（彼とは二度と会わないと決心した）

ニューヨークの風景

Coney Island　コニーアイランド （p.152, 最終行）

コニーアイランドは、ニューヨークのブルックリンにある庶民的な観光地・遊園地。本篇の舞台であるホテル・ロータスとは対極的な大衆の憩いの場であり、主人公ふたりがデートするには、格好の場所と言えます。

The Green Door

緑の扉

L et us think about adventure. You are walking along Broadway. You are looking into the shop windows and you are deciding which theater to go to. You are asking yourself, do I want something to make me laugh, or something to make me feel sad?

Suddenly a hand is placed on your arm. You turn to look deep into the eyes of a beautiful woman, wonderful in jewels and richly dressed. Quickly she puts into your hand a piece of hot——very hot——bread and butter. She cuts a small piece of cloth from your coat. She speaks one word and it means nothing to you. Then quickly she runs down a side street, looking back fearfully over her shoulder.

That would be pure adventure. Would you accept it?

■Let us think about 〜. 〜について考えてみよう。 ■ask oneself 自問する ■make 〜 laugh 〜を笑わせる ■make A feel 〜 Aを〜の気分にさせる ■look back over one's shoulder 肩ごしに振り返る

冒険について考えてみよう。ブロードウェイを歩いているとする。店のウィンドウを覗き込み、どの劇場に行こうか決めようとしている。そして自問する。「笑わせてくれるようなものを見たいのか？　それとも悲しい思いをするようなものを見たいのか」と。

　思いがけず、誰かの手が腕に置かれる。振り返って、宝石を身につけ、素晴らしく豪華に装った美しい女性の目をじっと見つめることになる。その女性は素早く、熱いそれも非常に熱いバター付きパンを相手の手に押し込む。彼女は相手のコートの布を切り取り、一言何かを言うが意味不明である。それから彼女はこわごわと肩越しに振り返りながら、わき道を走り去る。

　これこそ、正真正銘の冒険ではないか。そう思わないか？

No. Your face would turn red. You would drop the bread and butter. You would walk straight along, with one hand over the hole in your coat. This you would do, if you are not one of the very few in whom the pure spirit of adventure is not dead.

There have never been many true adventurers. You can read stories about men called adventurers. But they were really businessmen. There was something they wanted——a lady, or money, or a country, or honor. And so they got it. But a true adventurer is different. He starts without any special purpose. He is ready for anything he may meet.

There have been many half-adventurers. And they were great men. History is rich with their stories. But each of them had a special purpose. They were not followers of true adventure.

In the big city of New York, Romance and Adventure are always waiting. As we walk along the streets, they are watching us. We look up suddenly and see a face in a window. The face seems to interest us strangely. Or in a quiet street we hear a cry of fear and pain coming from a house where no one lives. A cab takes us to a strange door, instead of to our own. The door opens, and we are asked to enter. At every corner, eyes look toward us, or hands are raised, or fingers point. Adventure is offered.

■turn red 赤くなる　■walk straight along まっすぐに前へ歩く　■and so そこで、それで　■be rich with ～がふんだんな、豊かな　■look toward ～に目を向ける

いや、おそらくそうされた人は顔を赤くし、バター付きパンを捨て、コートの穴を手で隠しながらわき目も振らずにまっすぐ歩く。多分そうするだろう。ただし、真の冒険心を失っていない数少ない人間の一員なら話は別だ。

　これまでも、必ずしも正真正銘の冒険家が数多く存在したわけでなかった。冒険家と呼ばれる人たちの物語を読むことはできる。だが、実際は彼らは本当はビジネスマンなのだ。彼らには女性や金、あるいは国や名誉など、手に入れたいものがあった。そして、彼らは欲しいものを手に入れた。だが、正真正銘の冒険家はそうではない。正真正銘の冒険家なら、特にこれといった目的がなくても冒険を始める。彼は、遭遇するものすべてを受け入れようとするのだ。

　これまでにも、半ば冒険家の人たちが多数存在していた。そして、彼らは偉大であった。歴史は彼らの物語であふれている。だが、その全員には各々特別の目的があった。彼らは真の冒険家ではなかった

　大都市ニューヨークには、"ロマンスと冒険"が、常に存在している。道を歩いているときも、"ロマンスと冒険"に絶えず見つめられている。急に顔を上げると窓に誰かの顔を見ることになる。そして不思議と、その顔に興味が惹かれるようなのだ。あるいは静かな通りで、誰も住んでいない家から恐怖と苦痛の叫び声がするのを聞く。タクシーに、自分の家ではなく知らない家に連れていかれる。ドアが開き、入るように言われる。隅々から目が向けられ、手が上げられ、あるいは指差される。そこに冒険の可能性があるのだ。

But few of us are ready to accept. We are ready to do only the things we do every day. We wish to do only the things that everyone else does. We move on; and some day we come to the end of a long quiet life. Then we begin to think. Then, when it is too late, we are sorry that we have never known true Romance and Adventure.

Rudolf Steiner was a true adventurer. There were few evenings when he did not go out seeking something different. He was always interested in what might be waiting around the next corner. Sometimes adventure led him into strange places. Two times the cops arrested him. Again and again he discovered that he had lost all his money. One night, his watch was taken from him. But he continued happily to accept every offer of adventure.

One evening, Rudolf was walking slowly along a street in the older part of the city. Many people were walking along the street that night. Some were hurrying home. Others were going to have their dinner at some restaurant.

The adventurer was a pleasant and good-looking young man. By day, he worked in a music shop.

He walked quietly and watchfully.

■move on どんどん進む　■be sorry that 〜を残念に思う　■lead A into 〜　A を〜に連れて行く　■by day 昼間は

しかしながら、それを受け入れる用意ができている人はほとんどいない。通常、人は、日々のことにしか受け入れる準備が整っていない。みながするようなことだけをしたいと思っている。働き続け、ある日、平穏な長い人生の終末に到達する。そこで考え始める。それから、遅すぎるころになって正真正銘の"ロマンスと冒険"を経験しなかったことを悔やむのだ。

　ルドルフ・スタイナーは、正真正銘の冒険家だった。夕方になるとほとんど毎晩のように何か変わったものを求めて出かけるのだった。いつでも彼は、次の角あたりに何かが待ち受けているかもしれないと興味津津であった。ときおり冒険に導かれ、知らない場所へ出向いた。2度も警官に逮捕され、いく度となくあり金をすべて失くした。ある夜には時計を奪われた。それでも彼は冒険が提供してくれるものすべてを、楽しく受け入れ続けていた。

　ある晩、ルドルフはニューヨークの古い街の通りをのんびり歩いていた。その夜は、大勢の人がその通り歩いていた。ある者は家路を急ぎ、ある者はレストランで夕食を取ろうとしていた。

　冒険家は、人好きのするハンサムな青年であった。昼間は音楽関係の店で働いていた。
　彼は静かに、あたりに目を配りながら歩いていた。

He passed a busy restaurant and saw beside it an open door. Above the door a sign was hanging, a sign for a doctor's office. A very large black man stood at the door. He was strangely and brightly dressed in red and yellow. Quietly, he was offering small pieces of paper to those who passed by.

Rudolf had often seen such a thing before. The black man's small pieces of paper would have the name of the doctor in the office on the third door. Usually, Rudolf walked past without taking the paper that was offered. But tonight the paper was put into his hand very quickly. He kept it, smiling.

When he had walked on further, he looked down at the paper. Surprised, he turned it over, and looked again with interest. On one side there was nothing. On the other side were three words: "The Green Door."

And then, three steps beyond, another man threw down the paper the black man had given him. Rudolf picked it up. There was the doctor's name, with the street and the number. This was what Rudolf had expected to find on his own piece of paper.

■open door 開けっ放しの戸口　■those who ～する人々　■pass by そばを通る ■put into ～の中に押し込む　■turn ～ over ～をひっくり返す　■throw down 投げ 捨てる

にぎわっているレストランのそばを通り過ぎ、その脇に開いたドアがあるのを目にした。ドアの上には看板がぶら下がっていた。看板は医者の診療所を示すものであった。黒人の大男がドアのところに立っていた。その男は赤と黄色のおそろしく派手な服を着ていて、道行く人に小さな紙片をそっと渡していた。

　ルドルフは、以前にも、こういったものをたびたび見たことがあった。黒人の男の紙片には多分、3階にある診療所の医者の名前が書かれているのだろう。いつもは差し出される紙を受け取らずに通り過ぎるのだが、今夜、紙片はあっという間に彼の手に押し込まれてしまった。ルドルフは、笑いながらその紙片をそのまま持っていた。

　ルドルフは、さらに先に行ったところでその紙片を見た。びっくりした様子でひっくり返し、興味深げに再び紙片を見た。片面にはなにも書かれてなかったが、裏面には「緑の扉」という3つの文字がならんでいた。

　そして3歩向こうでは、別の男が黒人に渡された紙を投げ捨てていた。ルドルフはそれを拾い上げた。それには医者の名前と通りの名前と番地があった。ルドルフは、自分の紙片にも当然こういうものが書かれていると思っていたのだ。

The young adventurer stopped at the corner to think. Then he went across the street, walked further and returned across the street to the first side.

Now he again walked past the black man. Again he received a piece of paper. Ten steps away, he looked at it. There were the same words that had appeared on the first paper: "The Green Door." Three or four other pieces of paper were lying in the street where they had been dropped. He looked at them. Every one had the doctor's name on it.

Two times, now, adventure had asked Rudolf to follow. He was ready.

He walked slowly back to where the big black man stood. This time as he passed, he received no paper. The papers were offered to some, but not to all who passed. It seemed to Rudolf that the large black face looked coldly at him.

The look was painful to Rudolf. It seemed to say that he had failed. It seemed to say that he was not a true adventurer.

Standing away from the crowd of people, the young man looked up at the building. He believed that his adventure must be somewhere inside. The building was five-floors high. A small restaurant was on the ground floor.

■ask A to ～　Aに～するよう求める　■It seems to A that ～ . Aには～のように思える。　■stand away from　～から離れて　■ground floor　1階

青年冒険家は、角で立ち止まって考えた。それから、通りを渡ってさらに先に行き、また戻って通りを横切り元の場所に戻った。

　再び黒人のそばを通り過ぎ、また紙片を受け取った。10歩ほど行ってその紙片を見た。そこには、最初の紙にあったのと同じ「緑の扉」の言葉があった。3、4枚の紙片が通りの捨てられた場所に散らばっていた。ルドルフはそれらの紙片を見た。どの紙片にもさっきの医者の名前があった。

　もう2度も、冒険がルドルフを招き寄せているのだ。準備は整った。

　彼はゆっくりと、黒人の大男が立っている場所へ戻った。今度は、そばを通り過ぎるときに紙切れはもらわなかった。紙切れは道行く人すべてに手渡されているわけではなかった。ルドルフには、黒人の大きな顔が、彼を冷たく一瞥したように思えた。
　その様子はルドルフに苦痛を与えた。それは、ルドルフは失敗し正真正銘の冒険家ではないと言っているように思えた。
　彼は人ごみから離れて、その建物を見上げた。冒険はその中のどこかにあるに相違ないと思った。建物は5階建てであった。1階には小さなレストランがあった。

On the floor above that was a hat shop. Above the hat shop was the doctor's office. Above this were several signs, of dressmakers, music teachers, and other doctors. On the top floor, people seemed to have furnished rooms.

Rudolf entered the door and walked quickly up.

On the second floor he stopped. The hall was not very well lighted. There were two gas lights, one far to his right, the other nearer, to his left.

He looked toward the nearer light and saw a green door.

14

For one moment he waited. Then he remembered the cold face of the black man at the door below. He walked straight to the green door, striking it loudly with his hand. Then he waited to see who would open the door.

In the moments that passed then, he could feel the quick breath of true adventure. What might not be behind the wood of that green door! Bad men planning bad acts, or beauty in trouble, or death or love——anything might be there.

■one ～, the other … 一方は～、他方は… ■for one moment 一瞬 ■strike 動 打つ、たたく ■a breath of かすかな ■in trouble 困った状況で

その上の階には帽子屋が、帽子屋の上には医者の診療所があった。その上には、仕立屋と音楽教師それから他の医者たちの看板があった。最上階に家具付きの部屋があるようだった。

　ルドルフはドアを抜け、素早く上に上がった。
　2階で立ち止まった。廊下の照明はそれほど明るくはなかった。ガス灯が2つ、1つは右側の遠くに、もう1つは左側の近くにあった。

　近い方の照明に目を向けると、緑色のドアがあった。
　一瞬、躊躇した。それから1階のドアのところにいる黒人の冷淡な顔を思い出した。彼はまっすぐドアの方へ行き、大きな音を立てて手でドアをたたいた。そして誰がドアを開けるのかを見極めようと待ち構えた。
　それから一瞬、正真正銘の冒険の息吹を感じ取った。この緑色の木の扉の背後はどうなっているんだろう。悪人がよからぬことをしようとしているのかもしれないし、トラブルに巻き込まれた美女がいるのかもしれない。あるいは死とか愛とか、なにかこういったものがあるのかもしれない。

A soft sound was heard, and the door slowly opened. A girl not yet twenty stood there. Her face was very white, and she was very weak. She put out one hand and started to fall. Rudolf caught her and carried her inside and put her down on a bed.

He closed the door and looked around. It was very clean, but she was very poor. That was what he saw.

The girl lay with her eyes closed. But now she opened them, and the young man looked at her face. He had never seen it before, but he knew that it was a face he had always hoped to see someday. Her eyes were gray, her nose was small, her hair was brown. It was a face to make this a wonderful adventure. But her face was very thin and it had no color.

The girl looked at him and then smiled. "I fell, didn't I?" she said. "That's what happens when you don't eat for three days."

"What!" cried Rudolf. "Wait till I come back."

He rushed out the green door and down to the street. In twenty minutes he returned. Both arms were full of things from a food shop and from the restaurant. He put them on the table——bread and butter, cold meats, cakes, milk, and more.

■fall 動 倒れる　■put out ～を差し出す　■put ～ down ～を下に置く　■That's what happens when ～．～するとこうなるのよ。　■Wait till ～．～するまで待ってください。　■rush out 飛び出す

ひそやかな音がして、ドアがゆっくりと開いた。20歳にもならない少女がそこに立っていた。顔は蒼白で、少女の様子は弱々しかった。少女は手を差し出し、そして倒れそうになった。ルドルフは少女を支えて中に運んで行き、ベッドに降ろした。

　ルドルフはドアを閉め、あたりを見回した。掃除はよく行き届いていたが、少女はひどく貧しかった。彼はこのような状態を見て取った。

　少女は目を閉じて横たわっていたが、目を開け、青年は彼女の顔を見た。まったく見覚えはなかったが、いつか会いたいと思っていた顔であった。目は灰色で鼻は小さく、髪は茶色であった。彼女の顔は、冒険を素晴らしいものにしてくれることを約束していた。だが、少女の顔は痩せぎすで、血の気がなかった。

　少女は彼を見つめ、それから微笑んだ。「わたし、倒れたのね。3日間も食べていないと、こうなるのよね」

「なんだって」ルドルフは叫んだ。「ぼくが戻るまで待っているんだ」

　彼は緑色のドアから飛び出し、通りへ出て行き、20分もすると戻ってきた。両手には食料品店やレストランで手に入れたものをいっぱい抱えていた。バター付きパン、コールドミート、菓子、ミルクなどを全部テーブルに置いた。

"Only little fools," said Rudolf, "stop eating. You must not do things like that. Dinner is ready." He helped her to move to a chair at the table and asked, "Is there a cup for the milk?"

"There, by the window," she answered.

He filled the cup. "Drink that first," he ordered. "And then you shall have something else. And may I be your guest?"

He moved another chair to the table and sat down.

A little color began to come into the girl's face. She started to eat like some small wild animal that has been without food for a long time. She seemed to think it was not strange that this young man was helping her. Her need had been so great that she was ready to accept any help.

But slowly, as her strength returned, she began to tell him her little story. There are a thousand stories like hers in the city every day. It was the shop girl's story——not enough pay, illness, a lost job, lost hope. And then the adventurer at the green door.

But to Rudolf it was not a little story. It was a big story.

■help A to 〜 Aが〜するのを手伝う ■May I 〜? 〜しても構いませんか？ ■come into 〜に入ってくる ■one's need（人の）必要なもの ■be ready to 〜する状態にある

「おばかさんだけが食べるのをやめるんだ。きみはそうじゃないよね。ディナーの用意はできたよ」。ルドルフは手を貸して少女をテーブルの椅子に着かせて言った。「ミルク用のカップはある?」

「あちらよ。窓のそば」少女は答えた。

彼はカップにミルクを入れて「これを最初に飲んで」と命じた。「それから他のものを食べるんだよ。ところで、きみの客になってもいい?」

彼は別の椅子をテーブルのところまで動かしてきて、座った。

少女の顔の色が少し戻り始めた。少女は、長い間なにも食べていなかった小さな野生動物のような調子で食べ始めた。少女は、この青年が自分を助けてくれていることを不思議とは思っていないようであった。彼女には、なにもかにもが必要だったので、どんな助けも、即座に受け入れたのだ。

だが、しだいに力が回復し始めると、自分のささやかな物語を語り始めた。彼女のような話はニューヨークでは、毎日、数限りなく起きている。つまり、安い給料のうえに病気をして失業し、希望を失くした売り子の女の子の物語なのだ。そして緑色のドアに冒険家が現れた。

だが、ルドルフにとって、それはささやかな物語ではなく、大きな物語だった。

"And you suffered all that!" he said.

"It was really bad," said the girl.

"And you have no family or friends in the city?"

"None."

"I am all alone in the world, too," said Rudolf.

"I am glad of that," said the girl. And it pleased the young man to hear that she was glad he was alone.

Very suddenly her eyes closed. It was not easy for her to open them again. "I'm falling asleep," she said. "And I feel so good."

Rudolf rose and took his hat.

"Then I'll say good night. A long night's sleep will be fine for you."

He held out his hand and she took it and said, "Good night." But her eyes asked a question.

He answered with words. "I'm coming tomorrow to see how you are."

■none 代 どれ1つとして（～ない）　■all alone ただ独りで　■be glad of ～を喜ぶ
■fall asleep 眠り込む　■hold out （手を）伸ばす

「きみはそんなに大変だったんだ！」

「ほんとうによくなかったの」

「ニューヨークに家族や友だちはいないの?」

「だれもいないの」

「ぼくも一人ぼっちなんだ」ルドルフは言った。

「それならうれしいわ」と少女は言った。青年は、彼が一人ぼっちだと知って喜ぶ少女を見て嬉しくなった。

　突然、少女の目が閉じた。それから再び目を開けるのは、彼女にとって容易ではなかった。「わたし、眠りそう。とてもいい気持ち」

　ルドルフは立ち上がり、帽子を手にした。

「それではおやすみを言わなくては。夜の長い眠りは、きみのためにもいいことだよ」

　彼は手を差し出し、少女はその手を取って言った。「おやすみなさい」。だが、目はあることを尋ねていた。

　彼は言葉で答えた。「きみの具合を見に、明日も来るよ」

Then, when he was at the door, she asked, "How did you happen to come to my door?"

He looked at her for a moment and felt a sudden pain. What if those pieces of paper had been placed in some other man's hand? Quickly, he decided that she must never know the truth. He must never let her know that he knew that she had taken such a strange way to call for help.

"I was looking for someone else," he said.

The last thing he saw was her smile.

Outside the door, he stopped and looked around the hall. And then he went along the hall to the other end. He came back and went to the floor above and walked to the far end of that hall. Every door in the house was painted green.

He went down to the street. The black man was there. Rudolf showed him the two pieces of paper with the words, "The Green Door."

■happen to ～ 偶然～する　■what if もし～だったらどうなるか　■call for help 助けを求める　■look for ～を探す　■the other end 反対側の突き当たり　■far end 遠くの端

それから青年がドアまで行くと、少女が聞いた。「どうしてわたしの家のドアまで来たの?」

　彼はちょっと少女を見て、急に苦痛を覚えた。あの紙切れが他の男の手にわたっていたらどうなっていたのだろう? すぐに、彼は少女が真実を知る必要はないと考えた。少女が、こんなおかしな方法で助けを求めたことに彼が気づいたと、絶対に気取らせてはならない、と。

　「ぼくは他の人を探していたんだ」と彼は言った。

　やっと、少女が微笑むのを見た。

　ドアの外で立ち止まり、廊下を見まわした。それから、廊下のもう一方の端まで行ってみた。戻って上の階に行き、廊下の端まで歩いていった。この家のすべてのドアが緑色に塗られていた。

　通りへ出ると、あの黒人男がいた。ルドルフは、"緑の扉"と書かれた例の紙切れを2枚、彼に見せた。

"Why did you give these to me?" he asked.

"I give some of those and some with the doctor's name," the black man said. "I'm paid a dollar to give those."

"But what do they mean?" Rudolf asked.

The black man smiled. "There it is," he said. He pointed his finger down the street. "But you are a little late."

Rudolf looked down the street. There he saw a theater, and over the theater was a big sign, in electric lights. It said, "The Green Door."

In the shop on the corner near his home, Rudolf stopped to buy a newspaper. As he stepped outside again he said to himself, "I know that it was planned that I should meet her that way. I know it."

For Rudolf Steiner was a true follower of Romance and Adventure.

■There it is. あれです。 ■stop to ～するために立ち止まる ■step outside 外に出る ■say to oneself 独り言を言う

「なぜ、これをぼくにくれたんだい？」

「その紙切れと医者の名前のあるものを配っているんだ」黒人の男は答えた。「紙切れを配ると、1ドルもらえるんだ」

「ところで、これはどういう意味なんだ？」ルドルフは尋ねた。

男は笑った。「あれだよ」と言って、通りの先を指差した。「だけど少し遅すぎたな」

ルドルフは通りに目を向けた。通りには劇場があって、劇場の上には、電灯に照らされた大きな看板があった。それには"緑の扉"と書かれていた。

ルドルフは家の近くの店に立ち寄り、新聞を買った。外に出て、ひとりごちた。「あんなふうに彼女に会うことは、初めから計画されていたんだな。きっとそうなんだ」

そう思うのも、ルドルフ・スタイナーが"ロマンスと冒険"の正真正銘の追随者であったからであった。

覚えておきたい英語表現

　好奇心あふれる「冒険家」のルドルフ・スタイナーは街角で小さな紙片を渡されます。そこには、わずかに３語 The Green Door と書かれてあるのみ。勇気をふるってスタイナーが目の前の建物の緑色のドアを開けると……偶然と勘違いから開けたスタイナーの運命は？　こう書くとミステリーじみてきますが、運命や人生を分けるものはまさに紙一重、神（紙）のみぞ知るというところでしょうか。スタイナーの場合は、冒険心があったからこそロマンスを手に出来た（出来そうな）のですね。スタイナーが受け取った small piece of paper は、今でいうflier (flyer)「チラシ」と言うところでしょうけれど、flier には「無謀な冒険、投機」といった意味もあります。take a flier で「冒険する」という表現になります。Are you ready to throw away your success and take a flier on something new?「成し遂げた成功を投げ捨てて、新たな事業に挑む準備はできていますか」

There were few evenings when he did not go out seeking something different. (p.164, 7-8行目)
夕方になるとほとんど毎晩のように何か変わったものを求めて出かけるのだった。

【解説】ここでは、few と not の２重否定によって、強い肯定が示されています。つまり、この文章も直訳では、「何か変わったものを求めて出かけない夕方は、ほとんどなかった」となるところを「夕方になるとほとんど毎晩のように……出かけるのだ」と強調されている訳です。

182

By day, he worked in a music shop. (p.164, 下から2行目)
昼間は音楽関係の店で働いていた。

【解説】 このbyは期間を表わしていて、「……の間」という意味です。
The sun shines by day, and the moon by night. (昼間は太陽が輝き、夜は月が照らす)のように、by nightとペアで使われることが多い表現です。

And you suffered all that! (p.176, 1行目)
きみはそんなに大変だったんだ！

【解説】 sufferにはこの文章で使われているように、「〈苦難・損害・不快なこと〉を被る、受ける」という意味があります。また、suffer from「〈病気〉を患う、病む」も頻出表現なので、一緒に覚えておきましょう。

He suffered from toothache. 彼は虫歯で苦しんでいた。

What if those pieces of paper had been placed in some other man's hand? (p.178, 3-5行目)
あの紙切れが他の男の手にわたっていたらどうなっていたのだろう？

ここでは、What if（もし～なら、どうなるのだろう）の後の文が仮定法過去完了になっています。つまり、「過去のことだけれど、現実ではない仮定の話」をしているからです。また、What ifはif節に直接法がきて「～したらどうなるだろう；～したってかまうものか」の意味でもよく使われます。

What if I get out of here right now?
私が今、ここからいなくなったら、どうなるのだろう。

What if he fails in business!
彼が事業に失敗したってかまうものか。

English Conversational Ability Test
国際英語会話能力検定

● E-CATとは…
英語が話せるようになるための
テストです。インターネット
ベースで、30分であなたの発
話力をチェックします。

www.ecatexam.com

● iTEP®とは…
世界各国の企業、政府機関、アメリカの大学
300校以上が、英語能力判定テストとして採用。
オンラインによる90分のテストで文法、リー
ディング、リスニング、ライティング、スピー
キングの5技能をスコア化。iTEP®は、留学、就
職、海外赴任などに必要な、世界に通用する英
語力を総合的に評価する画期的なテストです。

www.itepexamjapan.com

[IBC 対訳ライブラリー]
英語で読むオー・ヘンリー傑作短篇集 [新版]

2013年 5 月 6 日　　初版第 1 刷発行
2019年 9 月 8 日　　　　第 3 刷発行
2024年 2 月 3 日　　新版第 1 刷発行

原著者　　オー・ヘンリー

発行者　　浦　　晋 亮

発行所　　**IBCパブリッシング株式会社**
　　　　　〒162-0804 東京都新宿区中里町 29 番 3 号 菱秀神楽坂ビル
　　　　　Tel. 03-3513-4511　Fax. 03-3513-4512
　　　　　www.ibcpub.co.jp

印刷所　　**株式会社シナノパブリッシングプレス**

© IBC Publishing, Inc. 2024

Printed in Japan

ISBN978-4-7946-0800-0